PROMISING PRACTICES

High School
GENERAL MUSIC

Edited by Mary Palmer, William O. Hughes, Michael Jothen, and Hunter C. March

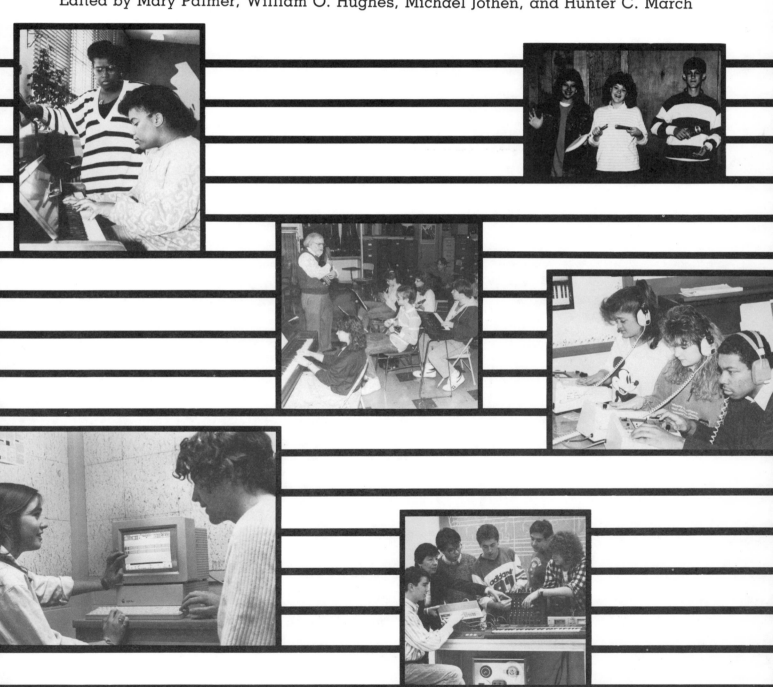

MENC MENC
MENC MENC
MUSIC EDUCATORS NATIONAL CONFERENCE

Photographs courtesy of the individual chapter authors. Cover photographs courtesy of Shirley Brown, Richard Bunting, Jeannette M. Hall, Austin Buffum, and Nancy Marsters.

TABLE OF CONTENTS

Editors

Mary Palmer, editor and compiler, is professor and coordinator of graduate studies in music education at the University of Central Florida, Orlando. She has taught public school music for grades K–12 and has taught in preschool, aftercare, community-based, and senior citizen programs. She has been active in the development of curricula and directed the 1989 Florida Governor's Program for the Study of Music for Gifted High School Students.

Palmer has published widely in professional journals and is an author of the Silver Burdett & Ginn elementary music series *World of Music*. She currently serves as a member of MENC's Publications Planning Committee.

William O. Hughes, editor, is professor of music education at Florida State University. He has thirty-two years of teaching experience, with ten of those years in the public schools. He has published widely: his publications include music education textbooks and articles for professional journals. He was a member of the Comprehensive Musicianship Project and a member of the Hawaii music curriculum team. His research centers on identifying age-appropriate materials for the high school general music student.

Hughes was founder and cochairperson of the first national conference on Music for the High School General Student, held in 1986 in Orlando, Florida. He currently serves as high school coordinator for *General Music Today* and as a member of the executive board of the Society for General Music. He is coeditor of the MENC publication, *Music in the High School: Current Approaches to Secondary General Music Instruction.*

Michael Jothen, editor, is supervisor of secondary vocal and general music for the Baltimore County (Maryland) Public Schools. As a composer, he has published choral compositions that appear in church and school festivals and concerts; as a choral conductor and clinician, he has directed concerts and assisted choral musicians in clinics, sessions, and workshops; and as an author, he has published articles in the areas of vocal and general music and has served as a senior author of the Macmillan Publishing Company middle/junior high series *Music and You.*

Jothen has had a wide range of experience in working with choirs of children, young people, and adults in school, church, and community settings and currently leads the adult choir of St. Michael's Lutheran Church in Baltimore, Maryland. He is a member of the board of directors of the Choristers Guild and chairman of the Professional Certification Task Force of the Music Educators National Conference.

Hunter C. March, editor, is associate professor of music and director of graduate studies in music at The University of Texas at Austin, where he teaches graduate and undergraduate courses in secondary choral and general music methods. He has presented workshops throughout the United States on choral and general music in the junior high/middle school.

March is author of several articles and of the Silver Burdett & Ginn *World of Choral Music*. He serves as the current chair of the Society for General Music.

Preface

Since 1980, twenty-seven states have enacted high school graduation requirements that include the arts, bringing the total number of states that currently include such requirements to twenty-nine. In order to meet the needs of the student who does not elect to participate in a performing organization such as band, orchestra, or chorus, many teachers and school districts are developing "general music" courses. Perhaps due to a lack of pre-service preparation, coupled with the lack of a burning desire to teach general music, many secondary teachers have difficulty developing effective music courses for general education. This book has been published as a step in the process of providing direction to teachers who seek to develop general music courses for high school students.

In order to identify promising practices in high school general music, inquiries were sent to the Society for General Music representative and the president from each federated state music educators association; announcements also were placed in *MENC Soundpost* and in the *Music Educators Journal*. From the many outstanding programs nominated, an MENC Committee selected ten to be chronicled in this publication. Although not detailed in the book, several additional programs are listed in the Appendix.

Developing musical understanding through active involvement with music is a theme common to the ten promising practices described here. Another commonality is the emphasis on students making choices—choices about instruments to play, compositional strategies, members of study groups, and so forth. Music as a personal experience is important in each of these programs. The teachers have capitalized on their own interests, talents, specialized knowledge, and personalities to develop unique and successful courses. It is apparent that teachers can design and implement popular and meaningful courses regardless of background, school size, student body, or financial resources.

The programs described in this book take place in widely varying communities. They include some that were developed by states, some instituted by local school districts, and others that were designed by individual teachers, but each program reflects the uniqueness of the implementing teacher. The goals set for the New York State *Music in Our Lives* course are approached in different ways by Bunting, Messina, and Trombley. Bunting achieves the goals through a course that emphasizes personal music making using traditional American music and folk instruments. Messina has developed a "music lab" approach emphasizing composition and using electronic equipment. Fifty percent of the students at Monticello High School enroll in Trombley's course, which includes performing, listening, and composing.

Frameworks set forth by the state of Florida are implemented in an ethnic music course described by Marsters. Music of the Western Hemisphere, including Africa, South America, the Caribbean, and the United States, is explored. The Baltimore County (Maryland) program *Music Perspectives* is represented in the work of Silverstein and Wharton. This course is based on the study of eleven compositions; concepts to be studied and classroom experiences are derived from the music. Hall extends her listening-based approach through the use of work stations and small-group assignments. Both Buffum and Modugno make extensive use of synthesizers, computers, and other advanced equipment in their differing courses. Additionally, Modugno describes a flexible approach to scheduling, which enables a large number of students to experience music. Brown effectively incorporates computers, audio recording, and video production in her group piano course, which is elected by 15 percent of the Berkeley (Missouri) Senior High School population. Finally, Hermanson describes experiencing the elements of music while creating radio and TV commercials in a camp setting.

Specific makes and models of equipment are sometimes listed under "Program Requirements": these references are an attempt to clarify information about the resources necessary for each program, and mention in this book is not meant as an endorsement by MENC or its affiliates.

These promising practices represent a sampling of the many fine programs that exist throughout the United States. The descriptions are intended as a stimulus to thought and not as comprehensive "how-to-do-it" course guides—they have been prepared to serve as a springboard for creative application of each music educator's unique strengths as a musician/teacher. It is hoped that music educators will continue to develop and share stimulating and usable approaches to the practice of high school general music and that this course of study may achieve the promise of helping music become an important part of the lives of more of today's students.—*Mary Palmer, Orlando, Florida*

Part One
FOCUS ON LISTENING

Goals and Rationale: Musical knowledge and understanding must be an integral part of the education of all high school students. This course seeks to involve participants in the study of significant compositions from different performance genres and historical periods. Emphasis is placed on enhancing student understanding of these compositions and the elements of music contained in each composition through the use of appropriate and varied instructional techniques designed to meet the differing needs of students.

Program Requirements: Equipment used in this program includes the Baltimore County *Music Perspectives Curriculum Guide*; bell sets; recordings; overhead projectors and transparencies; electronic keyboards; and audio equipment, including videotape, record, audiotape, and compact disc players. Additional equipment may be used at the discretion of the instructor.

Two school settings are generally used for instruction: a classroom setting with adjustments made for the use of audio, visual, and keyboard equipment and an instrumental and/or vocal rehearsal room. These settings are used as individual school space needs dictate.

CHAPTER 1

Music Perspectives

by Rebecca Silverstein and James Wharton

Baltimore County, Maryland, surrounds but does not include the city of Baltimore. The school system consists of twenty-one high schools (for grades 9–12), twenty-four middle schools (for grades 6–8), and approximately one hundred elementary schools (for grades K–5).

One credit in fine arts is required for graduation from high school in the Baltimore County Public Schools. Consequently, the music program offers a course designed primarily for nonperformance-oriented students. This course, Music Perspectives, focuses on providing participants with opportunities to experience and study selected compositions from the Baroque era through the twentieth century. Teachers of the course emphasize continued enhancement of the knowledge and understanding of the elements of music as presented in the general music program in grades 1–8 while helping the students to gain greater understanding of the cultural contexts within which the compositions selected for the course were created. High school instrumental and vocal instructors are encouraged to use varied instructional strategies depending on the unique needs and characteristics of a given student/class population.

PRACTICAL CONSIDERATIONS

Enrollment: Since all students are required to complete one full year of study in the arts for high school graduation, all Baltimore County students not enrolled in performance courses take Music Perspectives at some point in their high school program. As such, class enrollment may include varying combinations of students from grades 9–12 as well as students of divergent

CONTACT: *Rebecca Silverstein, music teacher, Woodlawn Senior High School; or James Wharton, music teacher, Catonsville Senior High School. Baltimore County Public Schools, 6901 North Charles Street, Towson, MD 21204. For information regarding the curriculum guide, contact: Music Office, Baltimore County Public Schools, 825 Providence Road, Towson, MD 21204.*

ability levels. Students in performing groups receive the required credit for Music Perspectives through their performing groups, in which the teachers present two units from the *Curriculum Guide* each year.

Equipment: Funding for the implementation and maintenance of the course is provided through the Baltimore County Office of Music. Unique needs of individual schools are funded by varied sources, including individual teachers, music departments, PTAs, and school-based funds.

Each semester, students are provided with an opportunity to listen to a concert performance, by the Baltimore Symphony Orchestra, of compositions selected from those they study in class. Students from all high schools are bused to the concert hall for the specific purpose of extending, reinforcing, and enhancing the instructional process through experiencing a live performance of works being studied. Program notes and verbal explanations are coordinated to support and enrich the content of the curriculum.

ORGANIZATION AND PHILOSOPHY

The *Music Perspectives Curriculum Guide* is divided into twelve units. The first unit provides an overview of the course; the remaining eleven center around the in-depth study of eleven concert compositions. The concepts presented in the course are derived from the music of the compositions, the background of the compositions and composers, and the relevance of the compositions to the consumer.

The objectives are based on the MENC philosophy as outlined in the publication *The School Music Program: Description and Standards* (Reston, VA: MENC, 1986). They are designed to ensure that students achieve minimal competencies at each grade level, and all objectives are stated in terms of three actions: perform, organize, and describe.

Performing, as used in the *Curriculum Guide*, refers to those skills that are related to the production of musical sound. They include the use of the body as an instrument, the use of the voice, the manipulation of environmental sound sources, and the playing of instruments.

Organizing refers to those skills that are related to the creation of music through the determination of the sequence of musical sounds. Those skills may be further divided into the spontaneous development of musical ideas through improvisation and the communication of one's musical intent through composition or arrangement.

Describing refers to the skills of listening to music and demonstrating understanding through fundamental movement or expressive dance; visual representation, including diagrams and abstract drawings; verbal description, including both image terms and technical terminology; and the use of traditional notation and contemporary notational schemes. It also refers to the skills of reading music; that is, of translating the score into sound and giving verbal descriptions using both imagery and technical terminology.

THE *CURRICULUM GUIDE*

Music Perspectives provides opportunities for students to grow in their musical experience, knowledge, and understanding, as well as in their attitudes toward music that is representative of varied style periods and performance practices. The curriculum focuses on a wide range of compositions that have been chosen for the course and must be taught. Specific musical concepts and vocabulary to be covered and the behavioral objectives to be achieved are provided for each work. The way in which these materials are presented, however, is largely left to the individual teacher. The *Curriculum Guide* contains a wide variety of call charts, organizers, reading materials, and musical excerpts (see the accompanying list of the guide's contents). Teachers can use all or some of the suggested developmental and assessment activities, or they can create their own activities. This flexibility is especially valuable in that it allows teachers to adapt the curriculum to all students in their classes, from the "gifted and talented" to the "intellectually limited" and from the "musically experienced" to the "musically inexperienced."

Curriculum Guide *Contents*

Throughout the course, emphasis is placed on assisting students in becoming more familiar with the musical and sociological characteristics of a given composition through direct experience with that composition. Teachers are encouraged to follow and use the instructional goals and objectives as stated in the curriculum guide and to develop and use supplemental activities. Also, multiple opportunities are provided in the *Curriculum Guide* for students to listen, perform, analyze, discuss, and evaluate the conditions pertinent to a particular composition.

Toccata and Fugue in D Minor: Johann Sebastian Bach

Concept: Tone color (pipe organ, dynamics)

Objectives:

- Given a recording of Bach's Toccata and Fugue in D Minor, the student describes the tone color and dynamic range of the pipe organ.
- To understand how tone color and dynamics are changed, the students "build" a pipe organ in class.

Procedure:

- Have a student touch the keys of a keyboard (with pistons to control the stops) that is drawn on the chalkboard. No sound is produced.
- Give soprano recorders to three students and teach each one to play a note: either B, A, or G. Instruct them to play when directed to do so by the "organist" (a student working at the keyboard that is drawn on the chalkboard). The organist then pulls the "Recorder 4" stop and produces sound by touching the keys on the chart—the cue for the students in charge of this "rank of pipes" to sound their instruments. Add a "Recorder 8 rank" by teaching other students to play the same three notes, an octave lower, on tenor recorders.
- Add other "ranks," such as Bells 4' and (at the upper octave) Bells 2'; Xylophone 8', 4', and 2'; Vibraphone 3', 4', and 2'; Violin 4'; Tri-toms 16'; and Timpani 32'. You can add another keyboard illustration, setting it to control the additional stops or coupling it to the first keyboard. Eventually all students become part of the "pipe organ."
- The organist tries many combinations of stops to produce different tone colors and dynamics. Invite students to discuss the differences.

• Have the students listen to a recording of the Toccata and Fugue in D Minor and describe the changes in tone color and dynamics.

Symphony No. 5: Ludwig van Beethoven

Concepts: melody (motive) and harmony (major and minor).

Objectives:

• Given the difference between a motive and a melody containing two or more phrases, the student describes motive.

• Given Beethoven's Symphony No. 5, the student describes the use of the motive.

• Given Beethoven's Symphony No. 5, the student describes the change in key from C minor to C major.

Assessment: As a developmental and assessment activity for this lesson, the teacher demonstrates occurrences of the main motive in the first movement and explains Beethoven's description, "Thus Fate knocks at the door." The teacher explains that the use of these words signals the approach of program music. Students listen to the first movement, concentrating on the constant recurrence and various forms of the motive. As they listen, the students circle each occurrence of the motive on a resource sheet.

Messiah: George Frideric Handel

In the lesson on Handel's *Messiah*, the students are given copies of the following sheet:

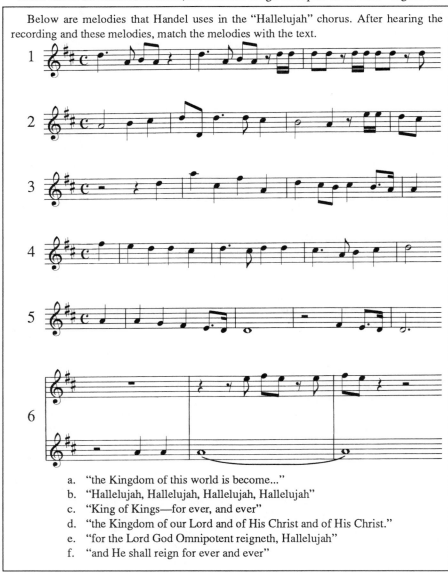

Below are melodies that Handel uses in the "Hallelujah" chorus. After hearing the recording and these melodies, match the melodies with the text.

a. "the Kingdom of this world is become..."
b. "Hallelujah, Hallelujah, Hallelujah, Hallelujah"
c. "King of Kings—for ever, and ever"
d. "the Kingdom of our Lord and of His Christ and of His Christ."
e. "for the Lord God Omnipotent reigneth, Hallelujah"
f. "and He shall reign for ever and ever"

***Don Giovanni*: Wolfgang Amadeus Mozart**

In the lesson on Mozart's *Don Giovanni*, the students watch a videotape recording of the opera's opening scene, in which the servant Leporello waits for his master, Don Giovanni, who is attempting to seduce Donna Anna. Donna Anna's father, the Commendatore, tries to intervene and is killed by Don Giovanni. They also read and perform (complete with action and props) the text of the following "class version":

Scene: (At night in the garden of a large house.

A man in a heavy coat is pacing back and forth.)

Lennie: Night and day I work for this ungrateful man! I eat poorly. I sleep badly. I'm sick of this work. While he's in there with his girlfriend, I'm out here in the cold being his "lookout." Oops! Someone's coming!

(He hides. A man and a woman rush out of the house. She is pulling at his arm as if trying to hold him back against his will.)

Anne: I'll never let you go unless you kill me.

John: You idiot! In this disguise you don't even know who I really am.

Lennie: (Aside, to himself and audience) What a racket. I see my fine "gentleman" has gotten himself into another fine scrape!

Anne: Help! Help, everyone! He's betrayed me!

John: Keep quiet! You're making me angry!

Anne: You're a turkey.

John: No, you're a turkey.

Lennie: (exasperated) This rascal's gonna be the ruin of me.

Anne: I'm not gonna let you get away with this. I'll come after you!

John: (to himself and audience) She really thinks she's going to destroy me!

(An older distinguished man enters the garden. He sends Anne inside.)

Father: Leave her alone. Defend yourself!

John: Go away, old man. I'm not gonna fight with you.

Father: So you think you can escape me!

Lennie: (quietly) I wish I could get out of here.

John: OK! OK! If that's the way you want it. Die! (screamed)

(They struggle and fight briefly. John kills the father.)

The students are then asked to complete the following page:

---

1. Read each statement and mark it "true" or "false" based on what you have seen and heard in class today.
   - ____ Both versions had a similar plot.
   - ____ Both versions were in Italian.
   - ____ One version had music, and one did not.
   - ____ Both versions had exact rhythm and pitch for each word.
   - ____ One version had an orchestra playing as an accompaniment.
   - ____ Both versions had the same number of characters.
   - ____ One version had a happy ending, and one did not.
   - ____ Both versions left you wanting to know what happened next.

2. List the names of the characters in both versions.

   Class   *Recording*

3. Read each question. *Circle* the words that are the best answers.

   What is the *same* about both versions?

   Basic plot   Melody   Number of characters   Accompaniment

   What are the main *differences* between the two versions?

   Story line   Music   Language   Number of characters

4. Answer the following question with one or two complete sentences: How could we make our classroom version more like the one on the recording?

Symphony No. 5: Ludwig van Beethoven (lesson plan for differentiated instruction)

To reach students of varying ability levels, the guide provides the following sample lesson:
- Primary concept: melody (motive)
- Secondary concepts: melody (Minor/Major); contour

Vocabulary: motive, movement, major, minor
- Lesson objective: Given the first movement of Beethoven's Symphony No. 5, the student describes the use of motive.
- Student objective (written on the board): Today you will find and play examples of the motive of Symphony No. 5 in the first movement. (In the previous lesson, the students played the motive and wrote a definition of the term "motive.")

Procedure:
1. Have the students write the principal motive of Beethoven's Symphony No. 5: Draw a staff. Use a treble clef and a duple meter signature. Starting on G, write the first four notes (the motive of the first movement of Symphony No. 5).
2. Ask these questions: What is the rhythm of the motive? What are the pitches of the motive the first time it is played? (Fill in the notes on a transparency as students answer.) Listen to the motive. (Play the motive with a C minor chord.) Is it a major or a minor sound? (Play the motive G, G, G, E♭ with a C major chord as a comparison.)
3. Have a student read the objective from the board. Review the terms motive and movement.
4. Have the students turn in their notebooks to the page titled "Beethoven, Symphony No. 5, Theme from the First Movement." Have them follow the score with their fingers as you play it. Ask them to count how many times they hear the motive.

Beethoven Symphony No. 5
Theme from the First Movement

5. Prepare the pages labeled "Beethoven, Symphony No. 5, Examples of Motive in the First Movement" by numbering the first page as measures 1–27. Have the students put the pages in their notebooks and list them in their tables of contents. Divide the class into groups and assign the groups the following sections: measures 1–12, treble clef; measures 13–20, treble clef; and measures 1–20, bass clef. Using bells, have the students practice and play together. Ask them to circle the examples of the motive.

Beethoven Symphony No. 5
Examples of motive in the First Movement

Assessment: Assign the second page (measures 158–68) and third page (measures 491 to the end) as homework for this lesson. Each page should have the direction, "Circle each example of the motive." Collect and evaluate the papers; discuss them the next day.

Reread the objective. Who played the motive? Who played the melody? How was the melody different from the first time we heard it?

Review: Bach and Handel

This lesson is presented after the preliminary unit on style, the Bach unit, and the Handel unit. The entire lesson is a review for a double-unit test on information from both the Bach and Handel units.

Concept: Baroque style

Objectives:

• Given information on Bach and Handel, the student describes similarities and differences between them using a Venn diagram. (See the accompanying example.)

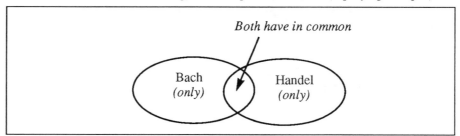

Venn diagram, with overlapping area that shows points in common between Bach and Handel

• Given excerpts from recordings of Bach's Toccata and Fugue in D minor, "Little Fugue" in G minor, Brandenburg Concerto No. 2, and Handel's Messiah, the student orally describes what he or she hears.
• Given vocabulary from these two units, the student matches words to definitions as part of a review.

Procedures:

• Have the students read and follow the directions from the screen, which ask them to list five or more facts about Bach and Handel.
• Distribute dittos of a blank Venn diagram.
• Help the students complete the diagram. Have them use the facts they listed earlier as well as other information they may discuss. (This is a pre-writing exercise for the essay question on the unit test.)
• Have the students put their lists and diagrams in their notebooks to study tonight for tomorrow's test.
• Ask students to identify the excerpts aurally. Lead a discussion on hints to help identify these examples.
• Have the students number a blank sheet from one to ten, and show a transparency of possible answers. Play ten excerpts, instructing the students to write one correct answer for each number as they listen.
• Distribute the "Vocabulary Review—Matching" ditto.
• Have the students use their notebooks to complete the vocabulary ditto.
• Try to take time for students to check their own papers through class discussion.

PERFORMANCE CLASSES

The *Music Perspectives Curriculum Guide* was developed to assist students in achieving minimum competencies in developing their understanding of the fine and applied arts and their historical contexts. Since many students elect to take a performance-oriented class in lieu of the "Music Perspectives" credit, certain Perspectives requirements are included in the curricula for these classes. Additional suggestions for performance groups, related to the twelve major units, are included in the *Music Perspectives* curriculum.

Each teacher of a performing group teaches a minimum of two units per year from the *Music Perspectives Curriculum Guide* to each of his or her performing groups. The same two units may be taught to each chorus, band, or orchestra in any given year. All of the required compositions are to be taught over a six-year period. Teachers of performing classes may use any or all of the developmental and assessment activities suggested in the individual units, and they are encouraged to develop additional activities specifically designed for performing classes. Choral, band, and orchestral literature is suggested to help students experience musical concepts through performance and study.

For example, in the unit on Igor Stravinsky's *The Rite of Spring*, teachers introduce the concept of rhythm (including polyrhythm and multimeter). The stated objective of the lesson is: Given examples of polyrhythm and multimeter from *The Rite of Spring*, the student describes polyrhythm and multimeter. A list of literature for reinforcing this concept and objective includes:

Choral Literature
- Bright: "Madrigal for a Bright Morning"
- Béla Bartók: "Two Hungarian Dances"
- Aaron Copland: "Stomp Your Foot"
- Norman Dello Joio: "A Jubilant Song"
- Howard Hanson: "Song of Democracy"
- Zimmerman: "Two Motets (This Day a Child is Born)"

Band Literature
- Bartók/Finlayson: *For Children*
- Bartók/Gordon: *From the "Children's Album"*
- Jager: *Third Suite*
- Leckrone: *Theme and Montage*
- Václav Nelhýbel: *Estampie*
- Václav Nelhýbel: *Festivo*
- Stravinsky/Wilson: "Berceuse" from the *Firebird* Suite
- Smith: *Emperata Overture*

Orchestral Literature
- Bartók/McKay: *Six Pieces for Younger Orchestra*
- Bartók/Serly: *Bartók Suite*
- Stravinsky/Isaac: "Berceuse and Finale" from *Firebird*
- Stravinsky/Isaac "Danse infernal" from *Firebird*

Goals and Rationale: Knowledge about customs, peoples, and cultures of other countries helps students see relationships and commonalities between the experiences of people around the world and their own lives. This course is designed to help students come to know and value selected world musics, to develop this knowledge into an understanding of their own music, and to learn more about themselves and others. It is hoped that the experiences of this course will motivate them to become competent world citizens.

The course familiarizes students with the music and cultures of the Western Hemisphere (those influenced by Africa and those of South America, the Caribbean, and the United States) and helps them acknowledge their own creativity and talents, develop a respect for the contributions of others, and acquire a base of knowledge to aid them in future musical decisions.

Program Requirements: A large classroom with nearby space for individual and group practice; listening facilities in the media center or library for out-of-class individual work; a large, current world map; a tape deck, phonograph, film and slide projectors, and screen; access to a video camera, monitor, and videocassette recorder; and access to an opaque projector, recordings, and cassette tapes.

CHAPTER 2

Musics of Western Cultures in Performance

by Nancy L. Marsters

Introduction to Music Performance—Selected Musics of the Western Hemisphere is taught in a portable classroom that can accommodate thirty chairs; therefore, enrollment is limited to that number of students. The student population is homogeneous and includes students of all ability levels from grades 9–12. The Introduction is part of the music program in a large high school enrolling approximately 1,750 students. At this writing, the band program enrolls 135; the choral program, 353; Keyboard I and II, 55; and Guitar I–IV, 90. Thus, approximately 32 percent of the total student body currently participates in music classes. The Introduction is taught only during the second semester of each year and meets daily, five times a week.

RATIONALE

In 1985, the Florida legislature mandated one-half credit in the performing fine arts as a high school graduation requirement. To meet that requirement, the Florida Department of Education designed a general music course titled Introduction to Music Performance. The state curriculum standards for this class were designed to be broad enough to allow each teacher to develop a course that both meets the standards and conforms to the teacher's specific professional strengths and interests. The state's framework for the course specifies nine goals for the students:

1. Play or sing musical works in a performance situation.
2. Identify common musical instruments visually and aurally.
3. Create and play simple musical passages.
4. Identify major music ensembles.

CONTACT: *Nancy L. Marsters, Leon High School, Choral Department, 550 East Tennessee Street, Tallahassee, FL 32308.*

5. Identify styles, composers, and characteristics of music
   in cultures and eras studied.
6. Identify varied ethnic or cultural music styles.
7. Explain the importance of music in everyday life.
8. Express personal musical tastes with appropriate vocabulary.
9. Identify career opportunities in music.

The introduction of any new course in a secondary school requires a great deal of support from the administration at both the building and county levels. In this case, a request to design such a course was presented to the county curriculum council after support from the local school leadership had been procured. After county approval, the course was immediately placed on the high school's list of course offerings for the following fall. The syllabus was then written under a summer grant from the Leon County School System. Implementation followed in the fall, and the semester course has been offered once yearly for the last four years.

Selected Musics of the Western Hemisphere is one course that uses an ethnomusicological approach to meet the state standards and to meet the educational needs of the students. Rapid technological advances in communication, involving all media, have made this a very small world. With each new invention, people find themselves increasingly aware of events in cultures other than their own. But understanding does not necessarily accompany awareness either on the part of music educators or in their students. For instance, recent national studies indicate a lack of student understanding of basic geography. A student who has no geographical awareness stands little, if any, chance of understanding much about the way people of different parts of the world live and think—or ultimately, of understanding what world culture has to do with us as Americans.

This class gives students an opportunity to explore the world and its music in a new way. Teachers and students can seek the roots of their own favorite current musical forms and, in finding them, learn something about the society in which they live as well as the part music plays in other societies. This course fulfills, at least in part, our responsibility as music educators to help today's students become competent citizens of the whole earth and to value musics of several cultures in addition to the music of their own.

GOALS

The purpose of this class is threefold: (1) to introduce students to a new and broader view of the music of the world's peoples, focusing on the cultures of the Western Hemisphere; (2) to stimulate students' creativity and, through classroom activity, help them develop a feeling of competence and a recognition of their individual talents; and (3) to provide a factual base for students' future music learning, listening, creating, and making choices as consumers.

The curriculum is divided into three basic areas: (1) Africa (this first section includes instruction in the classification of instruments), (2) South America and the Caribbean, and (3) the United States. Each area includes lectures, listening coordinated with the lectures, and at least one major hands-on activity. A fourth unit is designated for student presentations. The basic premise of the course is that the music of the Western Hemisphere is a result of the fusion of three major cultures—Native American, European, and African—and that music varies from place to place depending on the ways in which these cultures have interacted over the years.

COURSE STRUCTURE

Each fifty-minute class period contains a balance of lecture, listening, and a classroom activity such as performance or group discussion. Lecture and listening are used as a prelude to some type of performance or composition involvement on the part of the students. I take care to maintain open communication between teacher and students to create an atmosphere of free discussion, but take care that students separate facts from opinions, respect the rights of others when stating their own musical tastes and preferences, and refrain from derisive comments when other preferences are voiced. I ask the students to state musical preferences freely but ensure that they do not attempt to impose their preferences on others.

I have found that most class sessions can be handled easily in a single classroom. Some, however, require the use of small spaces such as practice rooms or outdoor areas adjacent to the regular room. It is helpful to have access to a tape deck, a phonograph, and a screen for films and slides. A video camera with monitor and videocassette recorder are very useful, and an opaque projector can be of occasional value. A large, up-to-date world map is a must.

USE OF THE LESSON PLANS AND LISTENING LOGS

Week 1: Introduction, definition of ethnomusicology (daily listening in the first week focuses on factors such as melody, harmony, rhythm, texture, ensemble); Cultures of the hemisphere; Music in American culture; Course outline; Terminology

Week 2: Elements of music, geography, listening, discussion; *Music of Africa* (film); Introduction to the world's instruments; Idiophones of Africa; Membranophones of Africa

Week 3: Aerophones of Africa; Chordophones of Africa; Student-made instruments played in class; Instrumental ensemble playing from rhythm charts; Ensemble practice

Week 4: Instrumental ensemble performance; Traditional music in African life; Traditional music of the Yoruba/highlife/Juju; Soukous, West African popular music; Guitar music of Africa

Week 5: Exam; Introduction to South America with general information on the Native American peoples; *Introduction to the Music of South America* (film); Intrusion of Western culture in South America; Spanish- and Portuguese-influenced music

Week 6: The Music of Spain and continued discussion of Iberian influence in South America; Argentina, Paraguay, Venezuela; Review for six-week exam, listening, and vocabulary; Six-week exam; Colombia, Ecuador, Surinam

Week 7: Brazil; Brazil—learning to samba; Quiz—South American dancing; Introduction to panpipe playing

Week 8: Panpipe playing; In-house concert of panpipe playing

Week 9: Introduction to the Caribbean/Cuba; Trinidad and Tobago: international influence; Jamaica, an introduction; Jamaica, international influence; Current reggae

Week 10: Mexico; Caribbean rhythm exercises with student instruments; Play back-up for Caribbean recordings; Review of South American and Caribbean music

Week 11: Continue review; South American/Caribbean exam; *Black Music in America* (film) [assigned reading]; *Yonder Comes Day* (film) [assigned reading]; Life of the American slave and related music

Week 12: European-influenced early American music; *Jazz to Rock* (filmstrip); Country blues; Jug bands, female blues singers; Urban blues

Week 13: Blues influence on later and current music; Student-written blues lyrics; Ragtime, New Orleans; Jazz as an aural tradition/Louis Armstrong; Chicago jazz

Week 14: Chicago jazz; New York jazz; Jazz piano/boogie-woogie; Kansas City/major bands to 1934; Whiteman/Gershwin/Ellington

Week 15: Tommy Dorsey/Bing Crosby/Glenn Miller/Benny Goodman; Bop-progressive/cool; Review; Jazz test; Soul/gospel

Week 16: Early rock; The Beatles, Ray Charles; Rock, the sixties, acid rock; Rock, the seventies; Rock, analysis of current styles

Week 17: Student presentations

Week 18: Course review, student presentations; final exam

Supplemental Lessons: Careers in music; The recording industry; Field trip to a local recording studio; How composers and lyricists make a living; Class discussion and classification of today's most popular music (for example, pop, heavy metal, and rap)

Excerpts from Course Syllabus. Reprinted by permission of the Leon County, Florida, School Board.

Each lesson plan is linked to a listening log. The two are coordinated and must be used in sequence, although substitutions may be made among the recordings suggested for individual lesson plans. The instructional sequence begins with African music (see the accompanying adaptation of the course syllabus). When study moves to South America, the student already has some familiarity with African forms, and as students begin to study the influence of African music on the already-existing musics of the Native Americans and Spaniards, they have the knowledge necessary to understand the new subject matter. The same is true when students begin to study the musics of the Caribbean and the United States.

I have numbered the recordings used in this course by curriculum area, not alphabetically. The listening log references in each daily lesson plan contain the number of the record in the discography, the side of the album, and the cut on that side. To eliminate handling records in the classroom, I pull together all cuts to be used in a specific lesson on one cassette tape. This facilitates the presentation and allows me to maintain better classroom control.

SAMPLE DAILY LESSON PLANS

The first lesson contains introductory information and exercises. As each name is called for the class roll, I ask the student to answer by stating his or her favorite kind of music, and I note their responses. During this class, I also establish class format and procedures. The students learn that there is a daily lecture on new or review items, that listening notes must be taken daily on recordings related to lecture, and that on days when instruments will be used, students should pick the instruments up before class begins.

I make the following comments on expected attitudes and behavior in class:
- Each individual (including the teacher) is entitled to his or her own musical taste.
- This class is designed to help everyone hear, perform, and understand not only new musics but those with which they are already familiar.
- *Participation is expected.* Statements of opinion are encouraged. Opinions must be recognized as such and separated from fact.
- Each individual has the responsibility to maintain total concentration during the class hour, *but he or she must not attempt to impose his or her personal musical tastes on others.* Derisive remarks (or sounds) concerning the music enjoyed by someone else will not be tolerated.
- In each segment of the curriculum, there probably will be music that some people enjoy, some are indifferent to, and others do not like. Everyone will find something new to enjoy (and might discover something new that he or she will want to avoid buying).

The lecture continues with definitions for the terms "music," "musicology," and "ethnomusicology," and the following listening instructions:
- Be honest.
- Identify whatever you hear.
- Comment on whatever you hear.
- Use legible writing, proper grammar, and accurate spelling in your log.
- Distinguish between fact and opinion.
- *There are no right or wrong answers.*
- All that is required in the first week's exercises is that you write and write extensively.

The last point is especially important, because the purpose of this week's exercises is to acquaint me as the teacher with what the students hear and how they describe it. From this knowledge, I can plan realistic lessons. Finally, I distribute prepared listening notebooks to the students. The listening log for this lesson includes the following selections:

"Every Breath You Take" by The Police

"In the House Blues" by Bessie Smith

"Addis-a-baba"; side B, band 6 on *East of the River Nile* by Augustus Pablo

Drum ensemble from Ruanda; side A, band 1 on *African and Afro-American Drums*

"Maple Leaf Rag" by Scott Joplin

"India"; side B, band 7 of *Pukaj Wayra*

"Mambo Lake" by the Westland steel band; side B, band 1 of *The Sound of the Sun*

"Take the A Train" by Duke Ellington

Juju music; side A, band 1 on *King Sunny Ade*

"Hound Dog" recorded by Elvis Presley

Note: Information on the less commonly available recordings can be found at the end of this chapter.

The Elements of Music and Geography (week two, lesson one)

This lesson begins with a discussion—continuing from previous weeks—of student listening notebooks. I try to make positive comments on what was written, and often make the following suggestions for improvement:

- Use complete sentences.
- Comments such as "that was weird" or "it was really bad" or "awesome" define nothing. Such comments should be avoided.
- Begin to compile a music vocabulary so that when we attempt to describe what we hear, others will understand more readily.
- Listen to the individual elements of the music as well as the overall effect.

A brief overview of the geographical areas to be studied follows, starting with Africa. This discussion touches on the general characteristics of the continent, a general description of the people, the history of contact with outside cultures prior to European colonizations, Islamic influence, and the influence of colonizing Europeans. We then discuss South America in its relationship to Africa as well as discussing its indigenous peoples, Asian influence, and history of European colonization and importation of slaves. The last topic includes information on the general routes of slave ships, the countries from which slaves were taken, and the intermingling of tribal groups.

Discussion of the Caribbean includes its indigenous peoples; its relationship to Africa, South America, and the United States; areas and time frames of white domination; and differences from island to island. In terms of the United States, the lecture includes mention of indigenous and colonizing peoples, the importation of slaves, differences between British-dominated and Spanish- or French-dominated areas, and current areas of strong ethnicity. Resources for this lecture include the books by A. Kebede and J. H. K. Nketia and *Black Music of Two Worlds* by J. S. Roberts, listed in the Bibliography at the end of this chapter.

For listening, the students are asked to listen to something that they heard last week, but to use a different way of describing what they hear; and to keep in mind the comments made about their listening notebooks at the beginning of this period. The listening log for the lesson includes the following:

- "You Shook Me" by Led Zeppelin
- "Black Mountain Side" by Led Zeppelin
- African guitar; side A, band 2 on *Music of Africa, Guitars 2*
- Calypso; side B, band 6 on *Belafonte: Calypso*
- "Sing, Sing, Sing" recorded by Benny Goodman and his orchestra
- Latin jazz by Santana
- Traditional bluegrass by Doc Watson
- An example of gospel blues
- Jazz-rock by Chicago
- "I Shot the Sheriff" on *Legend: Bob Marley*

Idiophones of Africa (week two, lesson four)

This lesson begins with a definition of idiophones—describing, defining, and giving examples (with pictures) of stamping, stamped, shaken, percussion (played with a nonsonorous striker), concussion (played by striking two sonorous objects together), friction (played by inducing vibration with rubbing), scraped (played by drawing a scraper over a serrated surface), and plucked varieties. I show pictures of all types and play listening examples. For this lecture, I use the book *Musical Instruments of the World* (see the Bibliography), displaying pictures from it to the students with an opaque projector.

The listening log for this lesson includes recordings of:
- Postal workers cancelling stamps; side B, band 14 of the recording that accompanies *Worlds of Music*
- Stamping tubes; side A, band 4 of *African and Afro-American Drums*
- Friction bow; side A, band 5 of *Music of Africa, Rhodesia I*
- Mbira tune; side B, band 4 of *Music of Africa, Rhodesia I*
- Six mbiras and a rattle; side B, band 5 of *Music of Africa, Uganda I*
- Loose log xylophone; side A, band 1 of *Music of Africa, Xylophones*
- The sixteen-note xylophone of Uganda; side A, band 2 of *Music of Africa, Xylophones*
- Two xylophones of the Congo; side A, band 9 of *Music of Africa, Xylophones*
- A Lionel Hampton recording (any selection will do)

Student-Made Instruments (week three, lesson three)

For this lesson, class members bring instruments they have made. These should be simple idiophones—have the students consider these tips when creating the instruments:
- Use only junk. Purchasing of supplies is prohibited.
- Provide for resonance. For instance, a hand-held piece of metal will not vibrate when hit with an old flashlight casing. Therefore, you should hang the metal with something.
- Shaken idiophones are very easy to make. If you choose this type of instrument, try to do something interesting with the container. Also, be sure that whatever you put inside the container won't rot before the end of the semester.
- *Label your instrument with your name.*
- *Plan ahead.* Don't wait until the final deadline. Have your instrument in class at least two days in advance.
- If you make something that is very soft-sounding, you can amplify it by adding some kind of resonator. An old coffee can or Quaker Oats–type container will work well.

When calling the roll, I have each student describe his or her instrument, detailing the method of construction. I then ask each student to play a simple, dictated rhythm, after which we classify the instruments according to type and regroup the students so they are seated according to instrument type.

I then introduce the Time Unit Blocks System (TUBS) of rhythm notation using the Africa/Ghana chapter from *Worlds of Music* (see Bibliography) as the model. Basically, this is a percussion notation in which a single line of boxes, each of which represents one unit of time (beat), is used to demonstrate a percussive part. A box that contains a dot represents a sound; an empty box represents a rest. We begin with simple single-line notation and continue until most students seem to have mastered it, move to an easy two-line pattern, and continue stacking rhythm patterns line by line. How far this is taken in the classroom setting depends entirely on the level of accomplishment demonstrated by the students—it is possible to continue indefinitely.

Each student should now create a rhythm pattern within a teacher-specified framework. This can be done using lines that are as long as appropriate for the students involved. Some students will handle twelve units easily; others do better with eight. Select two student-generated patterns, notate them on the board, and perform them with the class, using contrasting timbres from the constructed instruments. It helps if one of the timbres is somewhat bright and easy to define (for example, metal or glass). This exercise can be repeated with other student rhythms.

An interesting extension of this idea involves dividing the class into small groups of five or six. Be sure that the timbres in each group are varied. Each group should definitely have one metal instrument to carry an easily heard time-line. At this point, you need extra rehearsal space, such as practice rooms. Each group should be asked to develop a multilayered pattern, with each player carrying his or her own part. (Appoint a chairperson for each group, making him or her responsible for producing a copy of the group pattern and for running the rehearsals.) Groups should practice separately, with the teacher going from one to another to solve problems and help with performance. Put a deadline on this activity: at the end of the practice time, reassemble the class and ask the groups to perform for each other. If you have a melody instrument in the room, you can improvise over this background.

Jamaica: An Instruction (week nine, lesson three)

I begin this lesson by playing a series of taped musical examples with no introduction. We then discuss the music, focusing on overall sound, instruments, vocal style, rhythm, and lyric content. Only then do I identify the music.

A discussion of the roots of reggae follows, including information on current Jamaican politics, Jamaican history (including Columbus's landing, the Spanish settlers of the early sixteenth century, and the gradual dying out of the Arawaks; continuing with the first importation of slaves by Spain, the beginning of British rule in 1655, and the imposition of a plantation economy with more slaves. The discussion of Jamaican history concludes with the abolition of the slave trade in 1807 and the end of slavery altogether in 1834, the importation of East Indian and Chinese people on a contract labor basis, and the attainment of independence in 1962.

A discussion of religion in Jamaica includes information about the Church of England, the Zion revival, African remnants, and Rastafari. This relates to the Kumina, Convince, Zion revival, and Rastafari styles of religious music. We also discuss other musical roots in work songs including Digging songs (the examples "Imo Gal" and "Georgia Lyon" from the listening log) and plantation songs (example 5). Finally, we discuss Anancy stories and music based on folk tales. I use, as resources for this lecture, the books by Burnett and by Davis and Simon (see the Bibliography).

The listening log for this lesson includes:
- "Memories of the Ghetto"; side B, band 1 on *East of the River Nile* by Augustus Pablo
- "I Shot the Sheriff" by Bob Marley; side A, band 3 on *Burnin'* by The Wailers
- "Imo Gal" work song; side B, band 10 on *Black Music of Two Worlds*
- "Georgia Lyon" work song; side B, band 3 on *Caribbean Island Music*
- "Day-O"; side A, band 1 on *Belafonte: Calypso*
- "Matilda"; side A, band 4 on *Belafonte*
- "Bailo Song"; side A, band 2 on *Bongo, Bakra, and Coolie: Jamaican Roots, Vol. I*
- "Since Me Dead and Gone"; side A, band 3 on *Bongo, Bakra, and Coolie: Jamaican Roots, Vol. I*
- Revival Zion music; side E, band 24 on *Black Music of Two Worlds*
- "Rasta Rhythm" by Bob Marley; side B, band 5 on *Burnin'* by The Wailers

Jamaica: International Influence (week nine, lesson four)

This lesson begins with a discussion of some types of African-American Jamaican music: Mento (the first two examples in the listening log for this lesson) and Ska. We discuss the following elements of the latter form, which was popular from 1959 to 1965: rhythm and blues, Mento, the use of electricity, the use of fast tempos, the use of love lyrics (such as those in the third and fourth examples in the listening log).

Rock-steady, a style that was important from 1965 to 1969, incorporated slowed-down Ska, a strong, repeated tune in bass guitar, rhythm chords on beats two and four; and more serious lyrics (such as those in examples five and six of the listening log). Reggae, which was created around 1968 and is still an important style, uses the following elements: a bass tune, as in Rock-steady; elaborate percussion; social and political commentary in the lyrics. This style typically used rhythm chords on beats two and four, was recorded with rather sophisticated techniques (such as "dubbing"), and had an evident Rastafarian basis. (This can be heard in the examples by the musicians listed in the last item of the listening log for this lesson.) I use the books by Burnett, Davis and Simon, and Bergman as resources for this lesson.

The listening log for this lesson includes:
- "Wheel and Turn"; side C, band 15 on *Black Music of Two Worlds*
- "Mango Time"; side B, band 5 on *Caribbean Island Music*
- "Oh Carolino"; side A, band 1 on *Roots of Reggae* by The Jolly Boys
- "Get Up Edina"; side A, band 2 on *Desmond Dekker*
- "Shanty Town"; side A, band 1 on *Desmond Dekker*
- "Pretty Africa"; side A, band 5 on *Desmond Dekker*
- Two examples from recordings by Bob Marley, Desmond Dekker, Jimmy Cliff, Black Uhuru, Ziggy Marley, Third World, or other reggae performers. It is effective to have students bring examples from their collections, but it's a good idea to screen the lyric content before playing the tracks.

SAMPLE EXAMINATIONS

Exam 1 covers introductory terminology, the general scope of the course, and instrument classification.

Exam 1

FILL IN THE BLANKS. (two points per blank)

1. Name two types of idiophone and give an example of an instrument for each type.
   TYPE _____   INSTRUMENT _____
   TYPE _____   INSTRUMENT _____

2. Some aerophones have mouthpieces. Name two types and give an instrumental example for each.
   TYPE _____   INSTRUMENT _____
   TYPE _____   INSTRUMENT _____

3. Give two ways of attaching the head of a drum to the body.
   (1) _____   (2) _____

4. Drum bodies come in a variety of shapes. Name two.
   (1) _____   (2) _____

5. Name two types of chordophones and give an example of an instrument for each type.
   TYPE _____   INSTRUMENT _____
   TYPE _____   INSTRUMENT _____

6. In this class we will survey music from three continents. Name them.
   (1) _____   (2) _____   (3) _____

7. Much of North Africa has experienced Islamic influence. Name two countries that fall in this category.
   (1) _____   (2) _____

8. Black Americans came mostly from a specific part of Africa. Name two countries in that area.
   (1) _____   (2) _____

9. Name two specific things you have learned to listen for in music.
   (1) _____   (2) _____

DEFINITIONS. (30 points)
   (Ask the students to define terms taken from the following list):

1. music	7. Asante (Ashanti)	13. melody
2. musicology	8. idiophone	14. harmony
3. ethnomusicology	9. chordophone	15. rhythm
4. ethnocentric	10. aerophone	16. melismatic
5. acculturation	11. membranophone	17. syllabic
6. Yoruba	12. electrophone	18. vocable

CORRECTLY CLASSIFY THE TWENTY INSTRUMENTS ACCORDING TO THE CATEGORIES BELOW. (20 points)

A = AEROPHONE   E = ELECTROPHONE   M = MEMBRANOPHONE
C = CHORDOPHONE   I = IDIOPHONE

_____ 1. Clarinet	_____ 7. Xylophone	_____ 14. Trombone
_____ 2. Saxophone	_____ 8. Ukulele	_____ 15. Mbira
_____ 3. Electric organ	_____ 9. Slit drum	_____ 16. Oboe
	_____ 10. Triangle	_____ 17. Harp
_____ 4. Musical bow	_____ 11. Bass drum	_____ 18. Piano
_____ 5. Trumpet	_____ 12. Bass viol	_____ 19. Violin
_____ 6. Electric bass	_____ 13. Pipe organ	_____ 20. Guiro

People's musical judgments have been shaped and reshaped by their environments, which include such factors as nationality, ethnicity, community, family, education, and life experiences. People need to discover where they are, what they like, why they like it, and how they make musical choices. They can then broaden their range of musical understanding by accepting and acting on a simple premise: all music is made as a creative expression of the human personality and, because people respect that humanity, they must respect its artistic life. When music is perceived in this way, it becomes easy and even exciting to learn from people with different musical preferences. This does not mean that people will replace their own musicality with that of others, but rather that their own musicality will be open to enrichment and growth as a result of new experiences.

In teaching this course, I have attempted to set up an open and accepting environment that allows for new learning by teacher and student alike. Yes, I do most of the teaching and bring in most of the materials—but there is an important emphasis on student involvement and student initiative. Each time students create something new, they are sharing something from their own musical lives. Such contributions, acknowledged and appreciated by the teacher and other students, encourage more of the same. Before long, there is a classroom in which learning and teaching are seen as shared activities, in which each person has a responsibility to contribute and each contribution has respected value.

Success is evident when students come early so they can fiddle around with the junk instruments they've made, when somebody writes an original rap and isn't afraid to perform it, when the student who loves country music gives a presentation on Willie Nelson to a roomful of others who prefer heavy metal, or when the teacher decides that this is more fun than working.

Bibliography

Anderson, R., and G. North. 1979. *Gospel music encyclopedia*. New York: Sterling.

Anderson, W. M., and P. Shehan Campbell. 1989. *Multicultural perspectives in music education*. Reston, VA: Music Educators National Conference.

Bartholomew, J. 1980. *The steel band*. London: Oxford University Press.

Bergman, B. 1985. *Hot sauces*. New York: Quill.

Brown, C. T. 1983. *The rock and roll story*. Englewood Cliffs, NJ: Prentice-Hall.

Burnett, M. 1982. *Jamaican music*. London: Oxford University Press.

Davis, S., and P. Simon. 1979. *Reggae bloodlines*. New York: Doubleday.

Denisoff, R. S. 1982. *Solid gold*. New Brunswick: Transaction.

Epstein, D. J. 1977. *Sinful tunes and spirituals*. Urbana: University of Illinois Press.

Ewen, D. 1977. *All the years of American popular music*. Englewood Cliffs, NJ: Prentice-Hall.

Jones, B. 1983. *For the ancestors*. Ed. J. Stewart. Urbana: University of Illinois Press.

Jones, L. 1963. *Blues people*. New York: Morrow.

Kebede, A. 1982. *Roots of black music*. Englewood Cliffs, NJ: Prentice-Hall.

May, E., ed. 1980. *Music of many cultures*. Berkeley: University of California Press.

Megill, D., and R. S. Demory. 1984. *Introduction to jazz history*. Englewood Cliffs, NJ: Prentice-Hall.

____. 1977. *Music in American society, 1776–1976*. Ed. G. McCue. New Brunswick: Transaction.

Midgely, R., ed. 1976. *Musical instruments of the world*. New York: Facts on File Publications.

Nanry, C. 1979. *The jazz text*. New York: D. Van Nostrand.

Nketia, J. H. K. 1974. *The music of Africa*. New York: Norton.

Olsen, D., C. Perrone, and D. Sheehy. 1987. Sounds of the World—Music of Latin America: Mexico, Ecuador, Brazil. Reston, VA: Music Educators National Conference. (Audiocassettes with teacher's guide.)

Roberts, J. S. 1974. *Black music of two worlds*. New York: Morrow.

____. 1979. *The Latin tinge*. New York: Oxford University Press.

Shapiro, N., and N. Hentoff. 1955. *Hear me talkin' to ya*. New York: Dover.

Simon, G. T. 1967. *The big bands*. New York: Schirmer Books.

Titon, J. T. 1977. *Early downhome blues*. Urbana: University of Illinois Press.
_____. 1984. *Worldmark encyclopedia of the nations: Africa*. New York: Worldmark Press.
_____. 1984. *Worldmark encyclopedia of the nations: The Americas*. New York: Worldmark Press.
_____. 1984. *Worlds of music*. New York: Schirmer Books.

Select Discography
Africa
Africa Reports, 1984. UCLA.
African and Afro-American Drums. Ethnic Folkways FE4502.
Africa: Drum, Chant, and Instrument. Nonesuch H-72073.
Assalam (Vol. 1). Antilles AN7032A.
Black Music of Two Worlds. Ethnic Folkways FE4602.
Drums of the Yoruba of Nigeria. Ethnic Folkways FE4441.
Ju-ju Roots: 1930s to 1950s. Rounder 5017.
King Sunny Ade. Island MLPS9712.
Magic Panpipes of Mario Moreno. EMI/Angel S-38003.
Makeba. Reprise RS6310.
Music of Africa, Drums. Kaleidophone KMA 3.
Music of Africa, Flutes and Horns. Kaleidophone KMA 4.
Music of Africa, Guitars 1. Kaleidophone KMA 6.
Music of Africa, Guitars 2. Kaleidophone KMA 7.
Music of Africa, Reeds. Kaleidophone KMA 2.
Music of Africa, Rhodesia I. Kaleidophone KMA 8.
Music of Africa, Strings. Kaleidophone KMA 1.
Music of Africa, Tanzania I. Kaleidophone KMA 9.
Music of Africa, Uganda I. Kaleidophone KMA 10.
Music of Africa, Xylophones. Kaleidophone KMA 5.
The Nairobi Sound. Original OMA101.
Negro Folk Music of Africa and America. Ethnic Folkways FE4500.
Obo Addy. Avocet P-102.
Obo Addy. Avocet 5540-A.
The Soul of Mbira. Nonesuch H-72054.
Sound d'Afrique II. Island MLP9754.
Traditional Women's Music of Ghana. Ethnic Folkways FE4257.
Yoruba Elewe—Bata Drums and Dance. Ethnic Folkways FE4294.
Worlds of Music (accompaniment tape). Schirmer Books.

South America
Black Music of South America. Nonesuch H-72036.
Brazilliance: Laurindo Almeida. Pausa PR9009.
The Classical Guitar in Latin America. OAS 012.
Fiestas of Peru. Nonesuch H-72045.
Flute Music of the Andes. Olympic 6112.
Green and Yellow. Disco y Cultura 102-404-000.
Homenaje a Alberto Williams. OAS OEA014.
The Inca Harp. Lyrichord 7359.
Kingdom of the Sun. Nonesuch H-72029.
Los Mensajeros del Paraguay. OAS OAS006.
Mario Escudero: Classical flamenco. MHS 994/995.
Mexico/Fiestas of Chiapas and Oaxaca. Nonesuch H-72070.
Music of Mexico, Vol. I: Sones Jarochos. Arhoolie 3009.
Music of Mexico, Vol. II: Sones Huastecos. Arhoolie 3009.
Musiques Mexicaines. Harmonia Mundi HM57.
Percussions Bresiliennes. Le Chant du Monde LOX 74299.
Pukaj Wayra. Musik URS-5.
The Real Mexico. Nonesuch H-72009.
The Romeros Play Music for Four Guitars. Phillips 9500-296.
Sergio Mendes Greatest Hits. A&M SP4252.

Soledad Bravo—Cantares de Venezuela. OAS OEA-010.

Tudo Bem: Joe Pass & Dacosta. Pablo 2310-824.

The Caribbean

Belafonte: Calypso. RCA LPM1248.

Belafonte. RCA LPM1150.

Black Uhuru. Mango MLPS-9593-B.

Bongo, Backra, and Coolie: Jamaican Roots, Vol. I. Folkways FE4231.

Bongo, Backra, and Coolie: Jamaican Roots, Vol. II. Folkways FE4232.

Brasil. Pausa PR7156.

Burnin'. The Wailers, Island 90031-1.

Buscando America. Ruben Blades, Elektra 60352-1.

Calypso with the Lord Invader. Folkways FW6914.

Canciones Tradicionales del Caribe. OAS OEA005.

Caribbean Island Music. Nonesuch H-72047.

Desmond Dekker. Trojan TRLS226.

East of the River Nile. Augustus Pablo, Message 1003.

The Harder They Come. Jimmy Cliff, Island, MLPS9202.

Inti-Illimani 3. Monitor MFS787.

Inti-Illimani: Palimpesto. Redwood RR3400.

Legend. Bob Marley, Island 90169.

Milton Nasciemento. A&M SP4611.

Quinteto Rhupay, Folk Music from Brazil. Lyra 13083.

The Real Bahamas. Nonesuch H-72013.

Roots of Reggae. The Jolly Boys, Lyrichord 7314.

The Skatalites: Scattered Lights. Top Deck AL8309.

The Sound of the Sun. Nonesuch H-72016.

Third World. Columbia 44-05290.

Venezuela Musique Folklorique. Ocora OCR7A.

Part Two
FOCUS ON PERFORMANCE

Goals and Rationale: In the course "Music in Our Lives," students work with the "musical whole" of compositions to identify the raw materials of sound and silence (pitch, duration, volume, and timbre), the linear aspects of music (melody and rhythm), and the vertical aspects of music (harmony and texture).

By developing their skills in playing social instruments (guitar, keyboard, and recorder), students develop positive attitudes toward playing instruments, an awareness of the musical differences found in a variety of styles and cultures, and functional music literacy. By participating in composition activities, they work with musical elements to create a musical "whole"; they develop the ability to have increasingly sensitive aesthetic experiences. By completing a special interest project, they can expand their skills in the areas of basic musicianship, locating reference materials, communicating, organizing, and listening.

Program Requirements: The items necessary for this course are a phonograph or tape deck, recordings, a class journal for each student, a student checklist, and several guitars, keyboards, and recorders. A synthesizer, computer, and sequencer are also desirable.

CHAPTER 3

Music in Our Lives

by Ann Trombley

The course Music in Our Lives is the culmination of the K–12 general music program for New York State and is targeted for the general student population. It is open to all, and students can take this course to fulfill their art and music graduation requirement. The class roster includes students of varying abilities from all academic levels. Approximately 50 percent of the students in our high school complete this course by graduation.

The musical experience in this course is a positive one. Students develop a personal relationship with music as listeners, performers, and composers. We hope that they will experience the following outcomes and rewards as a result of that relationship: (1) a changed attitude in which they value music for all people, not just a select few; (2) a feeling of pride in their ability to make music; (3) a feeling of increased confidence in their musical judgments; (4) an interest in school and community music participation; and (5) a feeling of emotional satisfaction.

PHILOSOPHY

Music is a creative art and an expression of life, and should be an integral part of the education of children. Participation in music can reinforce skills in other areas, including listening, categorizing, organizing, and language. Furthermore, in studying musical elements by listening, creating, and playing musical instruments, students can develop an understanding of music and themselves. This understanding allows them to express themselves creatively and nurtures aesthetic sensitivity.

General music instruction is the core of the music curriculum. It stresses involvement of the learner in the development of musical concepts, which are refined and extended through direct application.

The teacher must provide a stimulating environment where music can be experienced and acted upon. The musical activities provided for the students should come from real-life musical

CONTACT: Ann Trombley, Monticello High School, Monticello, NY 02701.

problems. The hope is that this type of environment will motivate students to develop instinctive creative talents, the ability to make critical value judgments regarding music, and music participation skills as a means for self-expression. A goal of a comprehensive music program such as the one described here should be to help every student establish a solid and permanent relationship with music.

COURSE OBJECTIVES

By participating in this general music course, students work toward long-term goals through listening, performing, creating, and developing a special interest project. By taking part in listening activities, students are better able to identify musical elements and to discuss their contribution to creating music's expressive appeal. They are able to identify the "musical whole" of a piece, the raw materials of sound and silence (pitch, duration, dynamics, timbre), the linear aspects of music (melody, rhythm), the vertical aspects of music (harmony, texture), and feelings or ideas projected by selected examples of music.

By participating in performing activities, students can develop their skills in playing social instruments. Also, they develop positive attitudes toward playing musical instruments, an awareness of the musical differences found in a variety of styles and cultures, and functional musical literacy. By participating in composition activities, they develop the ability to create a musical whole and develop their aesthetic sensitivity toward musical experiences. Finally, by completing a special interest project, students develop their skills in basic musicianship, communication, organization, and listening.

CURRICULUM

The lesson plans are arranged in cycles. Each cycle includes activities designed to improve specific skills and the understanding of concepts. The approach is spiral in nature: the same concepts and skills will be used with increasing difficulty throughout the cycles. The lesson plans provide "hands-on" opportunities for the student by the incorporation of three basic activities—performing, listening, and composing.

One composition activity each year is designated as ongoing. In each cycle, the ongoing composition continues to be improved by the incorporation of additional means for control of musical elements. At the end of the year, the ongoing composition will include a variety of musical elements and will be a finished product that is notated and recorded for each student. The cycles show the development of an ongoing composition.

Each cycle is organized to introduce, work with, and reinforce selected skills and concepts. The first activity is a listening activity that reinforces the class discussions and gives students experience in recognizing the concepts in music they listen to regularly. The next two activities are performing and composing: these provide students with experience in manipulating the elements previously introduced. In the last activity, students evaluate their compositions with regard to the elements originally introduced.

CYCLE 1: BLUES COMPOSITION

Students who take part in this cycle learn about the three instruments available for year-long instruction (guitar, keyboard, and recorder), learn to differentiate between active and passive listening, and develop an awareness of the skills needed for composing traditional songs.

Skills: Students who participate in the listening activities learn to identify the form, timbres, and texture used in the blues listening example. They also learn to identify harmonic progression and phrase structure of the example.

By taking part in performing activities, students will learn to identify linear and vertical aspects of music (melody, rhythm, and harmony) by performing a chord progression using I, IV, and V chords on a guitar in one of three ways (selecting a method on the basis of their previous experience): plucking the root of the chord (single note), strumming the simplified chord, or plucking and strumming the full chord. They also perform a harmonic progression using I, IV, and V chords on the electronic keyboard in one of two ways (depending on their previous experience): playing the root of the chord and allowing the automatic chord feature of the keyboard to generate the remaining chord tones or fingering the full chord. Finally, they will improvise a melody on the recorder, using a given rhythm and a five-note scale. (The number of notes allowed and the difficulty of the specified rhythm can be modified, depending on student ability.)

Students who participate in the composition activities will learn to define and analyze the linear aspects of music (the association of rhythm and text, melodic contour, and phrase structure). They write lyrics for a blues composition and decide which of the text's syllables are short or long in duration (the exact rhythm for the lyrics is determined by the teacher). They also compose a melody from a given blues scale, using a form suitable for the original text.

Introductory activities: As preparation for the class, the teacher should discuss the word *timbre* with the students, explore several different timbres in the room, arrive at a definition for the word *timbre*, and listen to music brought in by the students, identifying the timbres used in the examples.

Listening Activity: St. Louis Blues

Play the first verse of the W. C. Handy blues song, "St. Louis Blues," and have the students complete a timbre checklist (on which they should check off the timbres they hear from a short list of instruments). Play the same verse a second time. Discuss the students' checklist answers in class, and have the students staple the listening lesson in their journals.

Next, play verse one of "St. Louis Blues" and indicate when the harmonic changes occur. Play the remaining verses and have the students point out the harmonic changes (that is, have them raise their hands to signal chord changes). Have students log the frequency of harmonic change in their journals. The actual progression is:

I	I	I	I
IV	IV	I	I
V7	V7	I	I

Repeat verse one. Have the students listen to the lyrics and identify the use of repetition and contrast. Label the form, and have the students listen to the remaining verses to determine whether the form of the text is consistent. Have the students log answers in their journals.

Play the first verse again, and have the students hum the melody and have them identify the form of the melody and label it. Listen to the remaining verses and determine whether the melodic form is consistent. Again, have students log answers in their journals.

Performing Activity: Guitar

Divide the class into several small groups. Give each group a guitar, and ask the students to describe everything they notice about the guitar. Speculate as to why the guitar is made the way it is. For example, ask them why the guitar strings are of different thicknesses and tuned to different amounts of tension. (They should answer that the string thickness and tension are varied to change the pitch and timbre of the strings.)

Introduce aural skills sequentially, in order of difficulty. First, relate these skills to a blues accompaniment by having the students pluck the root of the chords in the blues harmonic progression. The accompanying figure gives the tablature for the roots of the I, IV, and V chords of a song (such as "St. Louis Blues") that is in D minor. The tablature is for *your* information; it is not intended for the students at this time.

Second, have the students add a second note to each chord in the blues progression by plucking the root and strumming the remaining strings while you supply a steady beat (see the accompanying example).

This will not sound complete, but the students are merely establishing a process at this point. Finally, have students add the third note of the chord when they can manage doing so (see the accompanying example).

The students should pluck the root and strum the remaining strings while you tap a steady beat. If necessary, regroup the students so that they are all working on the same step of the procedure.

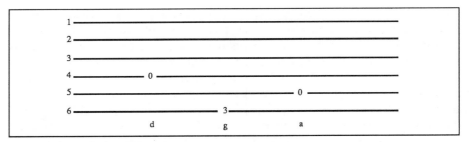

Tablature for D minor blues chord roots

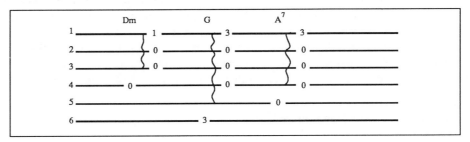

Tablature for D minor blues progression

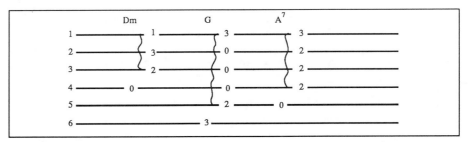

Complete tablature for D minor blues progression

Finally, improvise a blues melody while students play the accompaniment of the blues harmonic progression. All of these steps to learning a blues accompaniment are cumulative and should be added one at a time so that, on completion, the students are using all of the elements learned.

Performing Activities: Keyboard

Divide the class into small groups and give each group a keyboard. Show the students how to use the automatic chord features of their instruments, and show them the pattern of fingers on the keyboard for achieving the desired chords. Have the students practice moving from chord to chord (without rhythm) to practice the blues harmonic progression.

Select a rhythmic accompaniment preset. You can have one keyboard play this preset to supply a rhythmic pulse for the students' playing. Have the students clap the beat to the rhythmic accompaniment, and then have them play the blues harmonic progression with the rhythmic accompaniment preset while you clap the steady beat.

As the students become more comfortable with this task, have them repeat without your marking the steady beat. Finally, have the students repeat the accompaniment while you improvise a blues melody. The entire procedure can be repeated with full fingered chords for those students who desire the challenge.

Performing Activities: Recorder

Have students watch and listen to you so that they can echo patterns you create from a few notes of a blues scale. Continue creating patterns using more notes and different combinations of notes for students to echo. Create and play a phrase for the class and have them simultaneously create and play their own blues phrases; then, encourage students to perform their blues phrases for the class.

Have the class decide which two phrases they like best. Have the composers of those phrases teach their phrases to the class. Select an order for the two phrases (to follow an AAB form), and have the class perform the phrases in that order. Finally, have the students play the phrases again while you add an accompaniment on the guitar or keyboard.

Composing Activities

Preparation activities: Discuss the evolution of the blues song and relate it to political history. Listen to a blues song with many verses and discuss the text pattern, the number of beats in a phrase, and the placement of repetitions in both the lyrics and melodic line. Make up a class blues composition (lyrics only), following the textual pattern of your example.

Using the five notes D, F, G, A♭, and A, have the students make up melodies to go with the text, and encourage them to share their melodies with the class. Select some melodies for further development, and put the melodic phrases with the lyrics, following the pattern of repetitions in the listening example. Play the resulting composition for the class. (If there are students capable of playing an accompaniment, have them add one.)

Discuss the need to notate music so it can be performed at a later date. Add the rhythmic notation by having the students (1) divide the words into syllables, (2) repeat the text and decide which syllables are shorter in duration, putting flags on the stems for those durations (and notating other durations as appropriate), and (3) repeat the text, looking for syncopations and specified rhythms. (See the following example.)

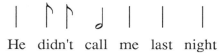

He didn't call me last night

Put a staff on the chalkboard, and write the rhythmic notation for the lyrics above the staff. Tell the students the note names for the five notes they have been using, and show where they are written on the staff, and help them notate their examples. Have the class play the example while you point to the notation on the board. (If you have a computer you can demonstrate how to save the composition in musical notation on disk and print out copies for the class.) Finally, have the students complete their own blues compositions following the previously explained steps.

Suggestions for classroom management: Divide the class into two groups. Have Group 1 compose while Group 2 practices their instrumental skills; then reverse the order. The group working on the instruments can chart their progress on their checklist. This arrangement allows for more hands-on time with the instruments.

Have the students work in groups of two when composing; they can support each other. At performance time, one can supply the accompaniment while the other provides the melody.

If possible, have the students enter their melodies into the computer for playback and printing. Most computer sequencer programs have a "step-time" entry function that allows students to make compositional judgments without being hindered by technical limitations. Also, computer-generated print is easier to read than most hand-written notation.

Evaluation Activities

Have the students listen to all the melodies composed in class (without lyrics) and discuss what characteristics are effective and not effective in a melody (a computer that can play these melodies will be helpful but not absolutely necessary; you or the students could perform them live).

Develop a checklist for a successful melody (have students log this list in their journals and post it in the classroom for use in future composition activities). Have the students go back to their own melodies and make changes based on the class discussion (have them log changes in their journals).

CYCLE 2: BLUES COMPOSITION

Students who participate in the Cycle 2 blues composition improve their performance skills, develop increased confidence in their ability to evaluate a melody, develop an awareness of the skills and concepts needed to compose a rhythmic accompaniment to a specific piece of music, and develop and refine their listening skills.

By participating in listening activities, students learn to identify the timbres used in accompaniment of the blues example, analyze the use of those timbres and their relationship to the rhythm used in the example played, and identify a simple syncopated rhythm pattern and other specified rhythm patterns as used in the blues example.

Skills: Students who participate in the performing activities develop the skill of using a synthesizer to "lay down tracks" by creating a rhythmic accompaniment for a previously composed piece (the original blues melody they composed in Cycle 1). Students who participate in the composing activities learn to analyze rise of sound and silence by creating a three-part rhythmic accompaniment that seeks a balance between the parts through the use of sound and silence.

Preparation activities: To prepare for instruction, the teacher should discuss the term *rhythm* with the students, echo-clap rhythm patterns and visually recognize notation for them, create a definition for *rhythm*, have students listen to music brought in by other students, and isolate rhythm patterns for study (clap and visually notate them).

Listening Activities: Timbre Identification

Prepare a checklist of timbres that includes some instruments that can be heard on blues recordings. Have the students listen to a blues composition and check the instruments they hear forming the accompaniment. In class, discuss the instruments mentioned and develop a list of those most frequently mentioned.

Listening Activities: Rhythmic Pattern Identification

Clap a variety of rhythm patterns for students to echo, and have them find the patterns you clapped from a selection of notated rhythm patterns. Have them listen to a blues composition and identify the patterns you clapped by raising their hand and stating the instrument playing them.

Have them clap other repetitive rhythm patterns. Then write the patterns out so that the students can see them notated. Finally, create a list of rhythm patterns frequently found in blues-style music and name the instruments that often play them.

Performing Activities

Have students select the instrument they would like to learn based on their experiences in the Cycle 1 performing activities. Teach students to play each other's blues compositions. Each student should play either the melody or a teacher-provided harmonic progression, depending on which part is more appropriate for the instrument chosen. Have them learn examples of varying levels of difficulty.

Performing/Composing Activities

Teach the students about your school's synthesizer. If no synthesizer or "drum machine" (percussion synthesizer) is available, use an acoustic drum set. List the names of the timbres available and demonstrate their sounds.

Demonstrate an example of a three-part rhythmic accompaniment in blues style.

Have the students independently create their own three-part rhythmic accompaniments for their previously composed blues melodies. Have them evaluate their accompaniment for use of stylistically appropriate rhythm patterns, timbres, and effective balance. Have them alter their accompaniments based on the evaluation.

Have them describe in writing the process they used to create the rhythmic accompaniment and attach it to the blues melody composed in Cycle 1. Teach them to put their compositions together by using a computer sequencer program and a MIDI-compatible keyboard or an acoustic drum set and a melodic instrument.

In their journals, have them evaluate the results of their efforts. This evaluation should include discussion of the timbres chosen and their relationship to the blues style, rhythm and its relationship to the blues style, and rhythm and its relationship to balance.

The order of teaching that you choose for these cycles must depend on the students' readiness. An extra cycle, devised to fill in the gaps, can be taught between the two basic

Blues rhythm accompaniment

cycles. This intermediate cycle could refine the concept of melody and the skill of melodic writing or provide the students with more experience playing the instruments. Another cycle could focus on identifying rhythm patterns and rhythmic composition skills. In all cycles, listening, performing, and composing activities should be provided for the student, and a hands-on approach should continue to be used.

CYCLE 3: BLUES COMPOSITION

Students who participate in blues composition activities continue to increase their level of confidence in their instrumental performance skills, to become aware of the skills and concepts needed to combine a bass line with a given melody, to develop an understanding of how a melodic bass line fits a harmonic progression, and to develop and refine their listening skills with regard to harmony and texture.

Skills: By participating in the Cycle 3 listening activities, students will become able to differentiate among textural styles of selected popular artists and to hear a melodic bass line within a given composition by accompanying the bass line of that composition.

Students who participate in the performing activities learn to perform compositions with accuracy in harmonic changes (through their use of harmonic instruments), perform compositions and recognize harmonic changes and sensitive phrasing aurally (through use of melodic instruments), and perform in an ensemble and demonstrate the ability to achieve balance. They also continue to develop technical and reading skills on their chosen instruments.

Students who participate in the composing activities demonstrate the ability to (1) understand the concept of chord construction by writing the harmonic progression to their blues songs and (2) analyze a chord progression and understand the concept of consonance and dissonance by composing a bass line for their blues composition.

Introductory activities: To prepare for the course, the teacher should discuss the terms *consonance* and *dissonance*; discuss examples of consonance and dissonance in art, clothing, music, and relationships; and create definitions of consonance and dissonance.

Listening Activity 1

Have the students bring in notated music or recordings of the music that they normally prefer. Listen to two pieces of music. Ask the students to compare and contrast accompaniment styles: How does the accompaniment support the melody? Is the accompaniment texture thick or thin? Does the accompaniment clash with the melody? Next, listen to the melodic bass line and ask them: Does it use as many different pitches as the melody? Does it clash with the melody?

Listening Activity 2

Play a recording of a blues composition (consider making your own recording so that it is in an appropriate key). Next, give each student or group of students a guitar and teach them to play the three pitches that are the roots of the chords. (See the previously given tablature for the chord roots in D.)

Play the blues composition two or three more times and allow the students to try playing an accompaniment using those three pitches. Walk among the students as they play and offer suggestions for the addition of more pitches to make up a melodic bass line. Write an ordered series of pitches on the board (working from student input) and ask the students to accompany the recording using the order of the pitches specified on the board. Have the class evaluate the success of their work.

Performing Activities

Arrange a student-composed blues composition for recorder, keyboard, and guitar. Be sure to include parts for each instrument that span at least three levels of difficulty. Have each student practice independently at his or her appropriate level: If a student finds the assigned level too easy, increase the difficulty of that student's part by assigning a new level. Have the students log their progress of completed levels on their checklists.

When the majority of the students have mastered a level, bring the group together to perform the composition as an ensemble. You can divide the class into two groups if the amount of equipment you have available is limited—one group can compose while the second group practices. Assign a student leader for the ensemble practice of the performing group. A full-class ensemble can wait until the completion of the cycle.

Composing Activities

Give the students written copies of the chord progressions for their blues compositions. Include the notes used in each chord and specify the root. Have each student refer to his or her copy of the rhythmic accompaniment (composed in the Cycle 2 activities), and have them each select and notate—using the letter names of the notes—the pitches that occur on the beat. (See the accompanying example.) The resulting arrangement can be programmed on a synthesizer, programmed into a computer, or performed live on an acoustic guitar, electric guitar, or keyboard.

Three levels of difficulty in a blues melody

Perform the rhythmic accompaniment with the melodic bass line created in this cycle. (If the bass line is programmed into the electronic equipment, the student will be able to evaluate it without interference from problems with instrumental technique.) Have the students listen to each other's compositions with all three parts (the melody, the rhythmic accompaniment, and the melodic bass line). Discuss the successes and failures of these

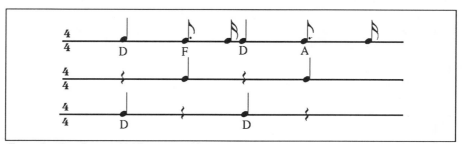

Example of student score (first measure)

completed works. On the basis of the class discussion, have the students evaluate their own compositions and log their evaluations in their journals. Their evaluations should include discussion of concepts addressed in all the cycles presented thus far. To increase the level of interest for the performance and composition activities, the students can plan a class recital to present their original works.

SPECIAL INTEREST PROJECT

Students choose topics on which they want to do a project, research their ideas, and share their findings with the class. They can choose to create a video, to present a slide show, or to create any method of public presentation other than an oral report. Participation in this project will help students continue to develop basic music skills, communication skills, organizational skills, and listening skills. Also, they can expand their musical interests and increase their knowledge on the topic of their choice.

METHODS OF EVALUATION

A critical component of education is evaluation. Through it, students and teachers can gain valuable information: Students become aware that they now perceive and understand concepts and ideas they could not grasp before. The evaluation tells students that they are learning—and tells them *what* they are learning as well. Teachers learn what concepts and skills the students have mastered and which concepts and skills need to be reinforced. This knowledge becomes the basis of the ordering of cycles and of decisions regarding the need for additional cycles.

The evaluation process includes three components: In self-evaluation, the students assess their individual progress (the use of student journals is helpful here). The formative evaluation is the teacher's ongoing assessment of the students' progress (checking students' journals and reviewing their checklists will be of help). The summative evaluation is the teacher's final assessment and will provide a valid measure of students' achievement (a final exam will be helpful). The evaluation process, like the learning process, should be a positive experience. If students and teachers participate in this process and a positive environment exists, both students and teachers will benefit.

Bibliography

Bunting, R. 1986. *Teaching traditional music and instruments: A classroom approach.* Bainbridge, NY: Traditional Music Materials.

Hume, C. 1975. *Creative etudes for the music class* (Available from the author, 31932 Watergate Court, Westlake Village, CA 91361).

Regelski, T. 1981. *Teaching general music—Action learning for the secondary schools.* New York: Schirmer Books.

Trombley, A. D. 1989. *Compose-perform-listen-compute: Making the general music connection* (Available from the author, 18 Lawrence Avenue, Monticello, NY 12701).

Goals and Rationale: This program is designed to provide students with opportunities to become knowledgeable about the elements of rhythm, melody, harmony, timbre, and form; to develop performance skills in instrumental and/or vocal music; to participate in a disciplined and directed group activity in listening, playing, singing, and moving; and to develop critical listening skills as a performer and a consumer. Students learn to employ music as a means of creative self-expression by using those elements that have been mastered, and they learn to recognize that various types of music reflect the historical and social backgrounds of different cultures and that all of those cultures have value. Finally, they develop the aesthetic awareness to make value judgments based upon knowledge and understanding; they enrich musical experiences through exposure to amateur and professional performers; and they assess the possibilities of music as a career.

The group piano situation allows students to be challenged and taught by their peers and to evaluate each other's performance and make suggestions for improvement. It also promotes healthy competition, which motivates students to achieve at greater speed. In addition, it provides opportunities for cooperative learning by allowing students to teach and learn from their peers.

Program Requirements: This program requires two Musitronic keyboard systems with twelve individual keyboard stations (including earphones and a teacher module) and two listening stations with twelve headsets. Digital equipment includes an Apple IIe computer with printer, an alphaSyntauri synthesizer, and a MIDI-capable Casio electronic keyboard. Two Tap Masters with rhythm tapes and a PitchMaster with ear-training tapes are used for developing musicianship. Finally, a video camera, a videocassette recorder, a television monitor, several acoustic studio pianos, and two grand pianos are used in the program, as are assorted workbooks and a collection of piano music representing various levels.

CHAPTER 4

Piano Lab

by Shirley Brown

Berkeley Senior High School, located in suburban St. Louis County, Missouri, is part of the Ferguson-Florissant School District, which serves all or part of eleven municipalities and a portion of unincorporated St. Louis County. Within these individual municipalities, the residents enjoy all of the advantages of a small town against the backdrop of a major metropolitan area with its diverse offerings. Approximately 15 percent of the school population elects Piano Lab.

COURSE PHILOSOPHY AND ORGANIZATION

The Piano Lab Program at Berkeley High School is divided into five levels: Piano Lab I, II, III, IV, and Honors. Originally taught as separate classes, Piano Lab now includes students from all levels in each class. The heterogeneous mixing of students at various skill levels has proved beneficial for all: the more advanced students assist the less experienced students, and the less experienced students are motivated by the performances of their more advanced peers.

Students are placed in one of three groups according to skill and ability. The groups take turns working at electronic keyboards with earphones, working at acoustic pianos, and completing work in music theory. While at the electronic keyboards, students follow a

CONTACT: Shirley Brown, Berkeley Senior High School, 8710 Walter Avenue, Berkley, MO 63134.

prerecorded lesson. Each tape takes the students carefully through the steps of the lesson, allowing time for playing responses. During this portion of the class, all students progress at the same speed. After completing the taped lesson, students move to the acoustic pianos, where they review and apply the information learned at the electronic keyboards, working at their own speed. After reviewing the lesson, they practice music chosen from one of the many books available.

The electronic keyboard lab

At the appropriate time, students move to the third phase of the class—music theory. They complete this portion of the lesson at their own pace, actively involved in working with programmed theory texts, a computer/synthesizer, and the Tap Master and PitchMaster musicianship aids. Although most instruction is individual, certain concepts and skills are introduced or reviewed using large group instruction. These skills and concepts include note reading, music history, dynamics, style interpretation, rhythm, notation, patterns, music games, ensembles, and music listening.

Throughout the program, individuals who need additional help are aided by the teachers, their group partners, or advanced student assistants. This individualized instruction calls for a great deal of structure—structure for facility of operation, for building a responsible attitude toward work within each student, and for overall accountability.

Student assessment is an important aspect of the Piano Lab program. Each student's daily lesson and progress is recorded on a chart, and his or her accomplishments and problems are discussed during regularly scheduled teacher-student conferences. Reports are issued to parents at the end of the first and third quarters, and they are discussed with the student during a conference. (Copies of the report are placed in the student's classroom folder and sent to the student's adviser.) At the beginning of each semester, I send each student's parents a letter explaining the history, goals, and schedule of the class. At the end of each semester, students receive a letter grade for their report card and take home a cassette recording of their playing to their parents. Parents return the tape with written comments.

All students in Piano Lab receive a grade of "incomplete" on their report cards for the first and third quarters. Grades are given for the class at the end of the first and second semesters,

Working on theory skills

indicating the students' progress during each semester in the three areas of Piano Lab. One of three grades is given: "superior," "acceptable," or "needs to improve."

Throughout the semester, students are encouraged to perform. They perform during periodically scheduled class recitals. In addition, students can earn extra credit by performing for friends, family, teachers, or one of the principals during lunch, and before or after school. They also have an opportunity to perform for large audiences during the annual Christmas and spring recitals. These performances provide important opportunities for students to build self-confidence and self-esteem. Guest artists—performers from local universities and professional jazz pianists—perform for the classes each year. In addition, a local composer teaches a workshop on improvisation each semester for all piano students.

Performing in recital

The following is a sample list of some class activities:
- Students sometimes videotape each other's performance. Class recitals are videotaped periodically for student-teacher review and evaluation.
- Advanced piano students visit elementary school music classrooms to assist individual students.
- Students make their own music videos, creating both music and visuals. Staff members from the school's audiovisual department assist with taping and editing.
- Students create their own compositions and learn how to copyright their work.
- A group of students put together a recital/video featuring the life and music of one composer. They perform the music and include historical comments between selections.
- During Black History Month, students present a recital featuring the music of Black composers. Each student researches and reports on the composition that he or she is playing as well as on the life of the work's composer. Students also participate in the Tri-M Music Honor Society's evening of "Black Performers: Then and Now."
- Students view professionally produced videotapes (such as examples by Victor Borge, about Thomas "Fats" Waller and "Duke" Ellington, or of the movie *Amadeus*).
- Seniors enrolled in Piano Lab present a senior recital. Participation is voluntary.
- Students create "albums" (floppy disks) of their songs on the computer and synthesizer; they also design a cover for their floppy disk album.
- Students attend recitals and concerts given by neighboring colleges and universities. This is strongly encouraged with the awarding of extra-credit points for attendance.
- The school district's piano tuner gives a lecture-demonstration on tuning. He also discusses what to look for when buying a new or used piano and discusses proper care of the instrument.
- Students demonstrate the use of computers in today's music education classroom for local civic groups.

SAMPLE LESSON PLANS

Keyboard Orientation and Facility

This lesson series is designed for beginning students. It is scheduled during the first part of the semester and can be completed in one or two weeks. It begins with keyboard orientation, in which the students:
- discover melodic direction (up/down)
- discover the high, low, and middle registers
- observe the visual pattern created by groupings of black keys
- play groups of two black keys (ascending and descending)
- play groups of three black keys (ascending and descending)
- play all white keys one at a time, starting with the lowest note and ascending to the highest note, naming each key as it is played
- observe how the black keys can help them find the neighboring white keys
- discuss the half-step/whole-step relationship
- discuss flats and sharps

In developing keyboard facility, students begin with G♭ and improvise a duet with a partner using only black keys. They are asked to begin in any register and move in any direction. We usually give students a metronome beat as a basis for their rhythm pattern. We ask them to play the following pentatonic melodies: "Amazing Grace"; "Merrily We Roll Along"; "Nobody Knows the Trouble I've Seen"; "Swing Low, Sweet Chariot"; "I'd Like to Teach the World to Sing" (verses only); "Hot Cross Buns"; and "Auld Lang Syne." Each student plays four of the listed tunes with their dominant hand and then four with the nondominant hand. After we discuss the differences involved in this exercise, the students play with hands together (doubling the melody) and finally play the melody in one hand and an ostinato in the other.

Helping a group of students

The Blues

This lesson series is for students at all levels, provided that they have already performed a blues tune. It takes approximately two weeks to complete. In it, students:

• discuss the harmonic structure of the twelve-bar blues:

I	I	I	I
IV	IV	I	I
V	IV	I	I

• find examples of blues progression in music they have played
• improvise (and, if possible, notate) a melody starting on G♭
• discover the iambic pentameter and AAB form of a typical blues text
• create a poem in iambic pentameter to fit a melody, adjusting the rhythm of the melody as necessary
• improvise a melody (using the keyboard or singing scat syllables) for the "break" between the phrases
• play the C-major scale and observe the half-step/whole-step relationships
• play the notes C, D, F, G, and A and identify the pentatonic scale. We discuss and compare the five-note scale with the diatonic scale. We then introduce "blue" notes in C-major, playing E and E♭ together. We discuss the effect of this technique and discuss the blues scale. The students then put together all components they have learned and record excerpts on a cassette tape or computer disk. We either have a listening session for all the tapes and disks or hold a recital of the compositions.

OBJECTIVES

In *Beginning Piano Lab,* the students are introduced to basic grand staff notation and are expected to be able to read traditionally notated songs (we check off the songs as students complete them). Students are given the keyboard note names to learn: they use the "keyboard notation" program on the computer and transfer their competencies to the piano.

The students study basic elements of music theory; they are introduced to simple chords and inversions and use their new knowledge to harmonize given melodies. They complete lessons in a music theory workbook and apply these lessons to the music (especially as concerns note values, counting, time signature, key signatures, and symbols).

The students are shown basic keyboard technique, including correct hand position, wrist movement, touch, and release. They are asked to demonstrate these techniques and are graded accordingly.

The students learn to use the Tap Master to help read rhythmic patterns and to use a system comprising the alphaSyntauri synthesizer and Apple IIe computer. They progress through the program disks *Simply Music* and *Alpha Plus*, receiving points on their completion.

Finally, the students learn to play for others and play in periodic class recitals. On completing the course, students are able to play the piano for their pleasure, having developed some basic skills in notation, theory, and keyboard techniques.

In *Advanced Piano Lab,* the students read more complex notation than they do in beginning piano. They play music that is appropriate to their levels; each composition is checked off for grading purposes. The student will play for others, including for Piano I students and their parents.

The students add more difficult accompaniments to a simple melodic line than those they used in the Beginning Piano Lab, including efforts to put arpeggiated chords or Alberti bass accompaniments to a simple melodic line. They learn to use a fluid wrist, good finger action, and proper pedaling technique. Each student is required to critique his or her (videotaped) performance. They are graded according to their level. They also learn to play duets or ensemble selections (with other students or with the teacher).

Students learn to use the Tap Master to help read rhythmic patterns and complete lesson tapes, on their level, with responses notated. They listen to keyboard recordings, videotapes, or

Using the computer in Piano Lab

tapes of varying styles when they study works in those styles (for example, the styles of Scott Joplin, Beethoven, and Clementi).

Students use the alphaSyntauri and Apple IIe for advanced theory or composition study. They progress through the *Alpha Plus* and *Metro Track* program discs, moving from one to the other as they complete each phase.

Throughout the program, the students use the piano as a means of self-expression and as an outlet for their emotions. The students increase their understanding of the art of music and its place in contemporary life. They develop a sense of pride in themselves as they experience the joy of creating their own music. Students are challenged to progress faster in group piano than they are in many other teaching formats. They usually want to play something they hear someone else play—this develops a competitive spirit in a friendly way. Through this, they develop a sense of responsibility as they work individually in a small-group setting to complete their lessons.

This program prepares students to play the piano during their leisure time, to play hymn tunes with simple harmonic structures, and to play for the enjoyment of other people: for parents, children, and friends. Their music study also makes them better consumers of music.

Goals and Rationale: Through active participation in music and music making, students can gain a positive attitude and develop a lifelong interest in music. Personal music making on one or several instruments—guitar, banjo, mandolin, Autoharp, recorder, pennywhistle, harmonica, or piano—emphasizes traditional American music and seeks to reach the increasing number of high school students who do not elect or cannot qualify for a specialized ensemble.

General and specific experiences offered in this course include a musical introduction via study of the dulcimer and work with musical elements, structure and form, standard and tablature notation, arranging, expressive elements, and basic theory. The many opportunities for enrichment include attending concerts, repairing instruments, interviewing area musicians, and completing directed listening assignments.

Program Requirements: The materials recommended for a class of twenty-five are eight banjos, ten guitars, three mandolins, two Autoharps, ten pennywhistles, and ten recorders. Additional strings, picks, and accessories also may be needed.

CHAPTER 5

Traditional American Music

by Richard Bunting

The Bainbridge-Guilford secondary school general music program is predicated on the belief that all students have the right to participate in the process of making music. To that end, the program is participatory in nature and addresses the dilemma of responding to individual needs in a group setting. Both affective and cognitive goals are integral components of the course structure, but the primary objective is to nurture in the students a positive attitude toward music and music making that will serve as a basis for lifelong interest.

THE MUSIC PROGRAM

The Bainbridge-Guilford school district is a small, rural district of approximately 1,050 students. The music department maintains strong instrumental and vocal programs that include band, orchestral, and vocal ensembles at all levels. These programs serve approximately 50 percent of the elementary students, 50 percent of the junior high students, and 40 percent of the high school students. The general music program includes classroom instruction in grades K–8 as well as the secondary program featured here.

All seventh grade (General Music I) and eighth grade (General Music II) students are scheduled for ten weeks of general music class each year. During that time, they study an instrument used in American traditional music (sometimes referred to as "folk" music). They choose from the following options: guitar, banjo, mandolin, Autoharp, recorder, pennywhistle, harmonica, or piano. (*Teachers can begin this program with any one instrument or any combination of traditional instruments.*) Extensive enrichment activities related to the music being performed are an integral part of the program. Junior high students who are interested may continue their study throughout the year during their study halls, when other general music classes are meeting, or during times when the general music room is open to all students.

CONTACT: Richard Bunting, Bainbridge-Guilford High School, 18 Juliand Street, Bainbridge, NY 13733.

High school students may elect to take General Music III at any time during their four-year tenure. Students can enroll for either a semester or a full year and can repeat the course (as General Music IV) if their schedules allow. They also have the option of working in the general music room during their study hall periods. This course fulfills the New York State graduation requirement of one credit in music or art. Since students in band, chorus, and orchestra fulfill this requirement through their ensemble participation, the majority of the students who enroll in the high school general music program do not participate in the ensemble program.

The total program currently serves more than 10 percent of the total student population and more than 20 percent of students who do not participate in the ensemble program. The high school general music class provides an opportunity for students to continue the study they began in the junior high school program. Students in the class begin study with the lap, or mountain dulcimer, both as a performance instrument and as a tool for learning basic music skills, basic music theory, beginning composition, and both general history and the history of American folk music. Classes and small groups of students perform and demonstrate performance techniques at club meetings, service organizations, senior citizen centers, hospitals, other schools, and teacher training sessions.

TRADITIONAL MUSIC GOALS AND OBJECTIVES

Historically, the role of traditional folk music in music education has been, at best, a beginning point from which students can be led to appreciate "higher" musical forms. Traditional music has not been viewed by music educators as a comprehensive vehicle for realizing the goals of most music education programs.

Recent developments in American society and in the field of education, however, have caused music educators to reassess the role of music education and, as a result, the role of traditional music in public schools. Such developments include (1) a decline in personal music making; (2) an emphasis on performance as a specialized, elitist activity; (3) increased costs of providing instruments for the relatively few players in high school ensembles; and (4) state legislative mandates requiring music and art instruction for all students. The profession has questioned the justification of music programs that have become too selective and too costly and that fail to respond to the spectrum of current musical needs.

The Bainbridge-Guilford Model for teaching traditional music meets the goals of both the New York State syllabi and the objectives of the district music program. It is the intent of this program that students experience participating, creating, and reporting; acquire performance skills, theoretical awareness, and historical awareness; and develop a personal identity with music and music making as well as a sensitivity to the variety of ways music can be made and enjoyed.

Student experiences: This program provides each student with the opportunity to have the following general experiences:
- A positive musical experience
- The value and pleasure of personal music making
- The enjoyment of group and ensemble performance
- A class designed to reduce competition and foster an appreciation of the accomplishments of others
- An exposure to the traditional musical heritage of the United States

The students experience the following elements of music:
- The function of melody, harmony, and rhythm
- Structure and form
- Standard notation
- Alternate forms of notation (tablature)
- Ear training and intonation
- Arranging (including work on introductions, interludes, endings, instrumentation, and so forth)
- Stylistic considerations (embellishments and other performance practices)

- Specific elements (such as pitch, dynamics, meter, phrasing, articulation, accents, tempo, key signatures, major scales, minor scales, modal scales, accidentals, repetition, and sequences)

The "hands-on" performance activities of this program should be augmented and enhanced by other activities such as the following:

- Attending concerts and festivals of traditional music
- Attending square dances or contra dances
- Taking part in the organization of a concert or festival
- Making instruments
- Repairing instruments
- Gathering information from filmstrips, films, television programs, and publications
- Preparing written and oral presentations of research on traditional instruments, music, performances, and performers
- Interviewing traditional musicians
- Making studies of family musical traditions
- Completing directed and general-listening assignments
- Attending performances and programs outside the class
- Composing music and lyrics in the traditional style

The teaching of musical elements is a continuous part of the program as students play independently and collectively. Concepts such as structure and form or performance practices are introduced to individual students or groups of students when they reach an appropriate level of readiness. Although this results in some repetition for the teacher, student frustration is reduced and new concepts are applied directly, significantly improving student comprehension and retention. The teaching of standard musical elements in this program also depends on the techniques of the individual teacher.

Singing: The secondary years are often a difficult time for encouraging students to participate in singing activities. Students will realize early on in a traditional music program that vocalizing the tunes is a necessity. The fact that playing the songs is the primary focus allows students to feel comfortable with their voices, and it has been my experience that they will join in the process of singing with a willingness that far exceeds that in other classroom situations. If the teacher will guide the development of this process in a nonthreatening way, while reducing the negative anxiety caused by competition and peer pressure, the students' expectations will change, and "singing along" will become a natural part of the class.

PROGRAM IMPLEMENTATION

To implement this course, the teacher must possess sufficient interest in this genre of music to master rudimentary skills on each of the instruments to be used. The teacher's level of performance need not, however, be advanced: *this program can be initiated with any instrument or instruments with which the teacher is comfortable.*

The teacher for this program should have the following skills:

- Knowledge of basic chords on guitar, banjo, and mandolin, and knowledge of basic chord positions on the piano
- Knowledge of fingerings for pennywhistle and recorder. Since the number of keys in which music for the course appears is limited (G and D to begin), this is not a difficult task. Pennywhistles come in different keys. One in the key of D will let you play comfortably in both G and D.
- Knowledge of basic strumming and picking patterns and techniques for guitar, banjo, mandolin, and Autoharp
- Knowledge of basic tablature for guitar, banjo, and mandolin. Tablature is a direct-response system that does not require that the performer identify the pitch being played.
- Knowledge of the tuning, care, and maintenance of the instruments used in class
- If the dulcimer is used, similar skill in playing techniques and in reading tablature

Many educators have chosen to initiate this model by beginning with only one instrument. If a teacher is already familiar with one traditional instrument (such as the guitar) and the school district owns or is willing to purchase a number of instruments of that type, then that instrument is the logical starting point for the course. If a teacher is essentially unfamiliar with all traditional instruments or the school district has limited funding, the best instrument to begin with is the lap dulcimer. This instrument works well for several reasons. First, it requires minimal teacher-training time. Second, reasonably priced dulcimers and dulcimer kits are available. Some have cardboard bodies—these instruments sound good and are very durable. Third, the lap dulcimer offers both melodic and harmonic possibilities. Fourth, it was developed in this country and is a unique element in the history of American music. Finally, it offers both instant success for the student and sufficient complexity for sustained interest.

Teaching the lap dulcimer

The school district must be willing to provide the necessary facility to teach this type of class and the storage space for instruments to be used. This program requires an investment of approximately $3,000 and a yearly allocation of approximately $500 for maintenance and replacement. These costs include:

- Eight banjos (with cases) $1,000.00
- Ten guitars (with cases)   1,100.00
- Three mandolins (with cases)   375.00
- Two Autoharps (with cases)   260.00
- Ten pennywhistles (brass, in D)   31.50
- Ten recorders (plastic, soprano)   35.00
- Strings, picks, and accessories   150.00

Costs could be greatly reduced by acquiring good used equipment or by soliciting a bulk order price. Students usually purchase their own pennywhistles, recorders, and harmonicas.

CONSIDERATIONS FOR SUCCESS

A class size of no more than twenty-five students is critical to the success of a participatory program such as this one. The inherent problems of large classes—insufficient time for attention to individual students and lack of flexibility—render that format impractical. In addition to this purely practical matter, we have identified several other considerations that are important in planning and preparing for a traditional music course.

Assume no student ability: One critical element in a participatory program that is often overlooked is the presence of a wide spectrum of student motor-skill ability. A perfectly legitimate program may falter because the implementation was not designed with this consideration in mind. This program begins at a point on any and each instrument where no previously acquired abilities and no particular motor skills are assumed.

Minimize competitiveness: Students today are forced to deal with competition in almost every facet of their lives. The therapeutic value of providing an alternative to a competitive view of education is reason enough to make the effort, and beyond this altruistic reasoning exists the practical consideration that the program cannot succeed in its primary goal of promoting a positive attitude toward music and music making for all students without this noncompetitive approach. In the general music program, class size is often large, positive peer pressure is minimal, and parental support is nonexistent—so we are faced with adopting unique solutions to the problem of reducing student frustration.

Accommodate the entire spectrum of student ability and readiness with choice, variety, appropriateness, application, and last but certainly not least, by making the music experience enjoyable. This course offers a number of different instruments for study and, within the limits of availability, the student is given his or her first choice.

The aspect of choice goes beyond which instrument to play. Providing for choice and the attendant responsibility implied in choice is a vital component of effective classroom management. If a program is restricted by funding or teacher preparedness in the number and variety of instruments it can provide, the educator involved will have to address the element of choice in other ways. Variety is critical to this program—not only for the sake of breaking routine that can lead to boredom for both students and teacher, but also because if one doesn't strive for variety, the total dimension of the program is unexplored. It is easy to become preoccupied with skill improvement and to lose sight of the potential for variety in such things as repertoire, format, audience, and the endless opportunity for teaching awareness through enrichment.

Appropriateness and application must be judged on a wider basis than that implied by the common term "relevancy." The relevancy of the program must be determined by more than the potential for immediate use of its content, and its worth must be evaluated on more than how well it aligns with youth culture. This program provides an enjoyable opportunity for students to learn at their own pace, to be evaluated in a noncompetitive way, and to acquire lifelong skills; in that sense, the students themselves perceive it as relevant.

Learning to play traditional instruments is fun. Unfortunately, many educators equate fun in the classroom with lack of content and lack of control. Some music teachers are guilty of offering loosely structured participatory programs because they fear that imposing guidelines will diminish the fun. These programs reflect poorly on "hands-on" or "action learning" programs where the enjoyment is the result of careful design, thorough organization, and skillful implementation.

Materials must be carefully designed, both structurally and visually, and must accommodate the spectrum of student ability. Many teachers attempt to utilize standard self-teaching or individual teaching materials in the classroom setting. This practice has two negative outcomes that are detrimental to the program. First, the class that uses these materials quickly becomes fragmented into small groups and individuals all working on different materials in the book. Second, classroom control and program effectiveness are further diminished because group playing, which is the core to success of any participation-based program, becomes very difficult. More advanced students become bored when asked to play easier material and less advanced students become frustrated because they do not yet have the skills to play along. Both conditions create management problems for the teacher—and the degree of diversity is directly proportional to the severity of the problems! In giving instrumental instruction in the classroom setting, we must change our approach to teaching technique. We cannot use new material for each step in skills acquisition: the materials must be redesigned so that technique can be taught using the same basic materials over and over again. In this way students of widely diverse abilities can play the same solo together with each student performing at a level that is related to his or her current skills.

For example, the accompanying music could be used in a lesson on recorder. If a student has only learned the note G, he or she can still play with the group by playing G when it appears on the chord line. When the student learns the note D, he or she can play the roots of all the chords used in the complete song. With the addition of the note B, the student can play melody 1. Melody 2 introduces the concept of quarter notes, melody 3 introduces eighth notes, and the remaining melodies introduce playing in duet and in variations using additional notes and more complex rhythms.

It is also important to consider the visual aspect of written materials for the classroom. Materials should be of sufficient size to insure readability from a distance, and they should be uncluttered to avoid confusion and frustration. It might seem a sensible procedure, for example, to eliminate melody 3 in the preceding sequence and simply show the basic melody and the duet part together. That type of shortcut, however, creates problems in the classroom, and when dealing with a large class of recorder players, it is best to solve in advance all the problems that can be anticipated since there will be plenty of the unanticipated variety to test the teacher's skill and patience!

A detailed teaching sequence for each instrument is important to both the teacher and student. It should not be viewed as a set of rigid requirements but should be thought of as a valuable framework for instruction and evaluation that offers the student an ongoing awareness of accomplishment. A teaching sequence should be based on advances in technique by small increments that can be introduced with minimal instruction time and practiced during the times the group plays together. The teaching sequence allows a student to attempt new skills during group playing sessions with the knowledge that he or she can "drop back" to a comfortable skill level if the new technique is too difficult. This is crucial to the teacher; not only does it reduce student frustration—it keeps the student from dropping out and becoming passive or disruptive.

A teaching sequence for guitar might be outlined as follows:

1. G and D7 chords—simple strum
2. Add C chord—simple strum
3. Add Em chord—simple strum
4. Simple strum using specific strings
5. Bass strum
6. Bass strum, alternating strings
7. Walking bass for $\frac{4}{4}$, in G
8. Other walking bass for $\frac{3}{4}$ and $\frac{6}{8}$, in G
9. Add Am, D, and A7 chords
10. Walking bass in D
11. *Introduce tablature*, simple melodies
12. Fiddle tunes and crosspicking
13. Melodies with chords

This is not, of course, a detailed discussion of the teaching involved. Considering, for example, only the first step, the teacher should check to see that the student is holding the neck of the instrument cradled at the base of the thumb with the bottom of the left hand held off the neck and the fingers curled high over the strings. For the first day or two, the student should strum with the thumb or the backs of his or her fingernails; the flat pick should be introduced only after the student achieves some flexibility in the left hand. The easiest way to describe the right-hand position with the flat pick is as a relaxed fist with the pick held between the thumb and first fingers. For the simple strum, the teacher should allow the student to strum all strings on all chords, strumming on the strong beats of each measure. Strumming should take place at the edge of the sound hole toward the bridge: this keeps the hand from covering the sound hole.

The teacher should have the student strum in tempo, without stopping, even if the left hand does not change "in time." (It is difficult to break the habit of stopping the right hand while the left hand "finds" the chord.) If continuing to strum while "finding" the chord is a problem, another solution to the problem is to have the student leave out the beat before the chord change, thereby allowing sufficient time to make the shift in tempo.

In the shift from G to D7, the first finger is the target finger. Have the student practice what that finger must do by itself. In all chord shifts the student's ability to visualize what the next chord looks like greatly facilitates the coordination. Have the students practice shifting from G to D7 to G. The G to D7 shift cannot be executed comfortably without shifting the hand up and down the neck. Ideally (eventually) the fingers should lift simultaneously and arrive at the new chord position simultaneously.

A similar detailed, comprehensive teaching sequence should be developed for each instrument used in the program with the attending materials being cross-referenced for group playing. If this is accomplished, every student, regardless of previous experience or innate ability, will have the opportunity to experience music making with the group from his or her first day with the program to the last.

Preparing students to begin seems a rudimentary concern, but I have found this to be a major shortcoming in the process of implementation. Part of the problem may be that those of us who teach secondary general music are not accustomed to anticipating the physical and behavioral problems that will interfere with instrumental instruction in the classroom setting. For example, I have found that simply passing out pennywhistles to a group of students does not work. I have had better success by preparing the students with finger-training on sticks shaped to the same size as the instruments. In using these sticks, I add dots where the finger holes would be on the second day of class; I have the students practice on the pennywhistles (but with the mouthpieces taped shut) on the third day of class, and ask them to play on the fourth day of class. Without this preparation, my students would not have enjoyed the same level of success.

Practice begins as a group activity and progresses to the state of an individual activity. The amount of time required for group practice prior to providing for individual practice varies greatly from group to group. In my experience with seventh and eighth graders in ten-week blocks of instruction, the time necessary to achieve proper readiness for individual work has ranged from one day to more than three weeks.

It is helpful to remember that group practice is practice—not a rehearsal. Music educators are trained, both by experience and methodology, that group practice (rehearsal) is the time when the teacher (conductor) does his or her best to bring the performers in line with a predetermined musical conception. In the type of group instrumental instruction proposed by this program, however, group practice is the time when each student works on his or her current level of technique.

The difference is fundamental and manifests itself in two dramatic ways: first, the sound of the ensemble is not a primary concept; and second, the teacher must exercise the creativity necessary to accomplish sufficient repetition for the acquisition of skills. The process of group playing cannot be sequenced as definitively as instrumental technique because the classroom variables are too numerous. There is, however, a logical order for introducing performance devices that will create interest in repetition.

Introductions

From the first time the group plays together some method of preparing the piece must be established. Initially the teacher will "count off" or play an introduction to a song. As soon as possible this responsibility should be transferred to the students. All introductions should be related to the strumming pulse, not "beats" per measure. (A simple introduction to a $\frac{4}{4}$ in G major that has no pick-up notes would be four G chords strummed in tempo.) This introduction should be adjusted to accommodate songs with pick-up notes. As the students' abilities increase, introductions can be created using bass strums, picking patterns, bass walks, or appropriate fragments of songs or solos.

Endings

As with introductions, endings must be kept simple at first, and can increase with complexity in accordance with the students' abilities. The easiest way to produce a satisfying ending in any key is to simply add a V–I cadence. The "shave and a haircut" ending is one of the best known, and students who are familiar with the fast V–I ending can learn it quite quickly. When students have learned how to end a song, the next major step is to learn how to continue on for additional verses, adding the ending after the final verse.

Interludes

Interludes between the verses of a song can be created in the same manner as introductions and endings. These interludes can also be played by separate instruments or small groups, and can serve as an additional element of focus during group practice. "Breaks" during songs (in which a melodic note is held for an extended time) can also be used.

Instrumentation

When students acquire the ability to repeat a song without stopping, the concept of varying instrumentation can be introduced. The number of possible combinations of instruments and/or individuals in any class is so great that creative use of this device is one of the most effective means for sustaining interest in group playing. An added dimension to instrumentation is to vary the techniques used from verse to verse. For example, a guitar or mandolin player could go from simple strum to bass strum, or a banjo player from basic stroke to double thumb. Ensemble playing concepts, such as balance, can be introduced from the beginning of group playing, but they are addressed more easily when students begin to deal with instrumentation.

A varied ensemble

Interpretation

Since class or ensemble development is so varied, it is difficult to say at what point it becomes feasible to deal with interpretive matters such as dynamics, tempo, phrasing, and articulation. Interpretive elements should, however, be addressed one at a time and applied from the largest musical component to the smallest. Dynamic changes (abrupt or gradual) should first occur from verse to verse, then section to section, and finally phrase to phrase.

Arranging

The development of arranging in class performance should ultimately lead to independent student work in this activity. The progression is most easily visualized as three distinct steps: Step one is characterized by teacher input with teacher control to create exposure to various elements. Step two uses student input with teacher control to learn techniques of applying the elements, and step three is based on student input with student control to practice the creative application of the elements. When students are properly prepared for it, they create their own arrangements in small groups. This process of small groups creating their own arrangements for performance is one of the most rewarding outcomes of this program.

EVALUATION

Students at the secondary level face the reality that their level of preparedness and innate aptitude drastically affect their ability to compete for academic success. If music educators are truly interested in helping all students discover that music and music making can be a rewarding part of their lives, then the general music program should be a place where grading is based on student effort.

A goal sheet should be kept for each student, showing what the student is working on and the time allotted for completing that work. I suggest printing a sheet that lists all the songs used in the class and provides a place for the teacher to note what techniques are to be used with specific songs (see example at the end of this section). If, for example, a beginning guitar student is to play some songs using simple strumming technique, the teacher can indicate "s.s." after the title as it appears on the sheet.

When the student has successfully "passed" a song, he or she can indicate that fact on the sheet and enter the date. If students participate in the record keeping, they are constantly aware of what they have accomplished, what they are to do next, and how much time they have to do it. It also frees the teacher to move about the room more quickly, providing more time to work with students. The time period for completion of a goal sheet need not exceed one week. Students should be encouraged to complete these sheets as quickly as possible. Whenever a student completes a sheet prior to or on the target date, he or she can be given an A (or a numerical equivalent) for effort and immediately begin work on the next sheet. If a student fails to complete a goal sheet in the allotted time, his or her grade is lowered accordingly and the incomplete work becomes part of the next sheet.

Students will complete the course with varying quantities and qualities of accomplishment. The teacher must determine how this variation among individuals will be figured in the grading procedure. After working with the program for a time, teachers will become more efficient at evaluating individual students and projecting the amount of time needed to accomplish specific tasks.

Using a short-term goal sheet provides a vehicle for giving credit for the practice necessary for the development of sound technique. A beginning guitar student, for instance, will usually be able to demonstrate the G to D7 chord shift in a short period. Their readiness to move on to the next aspect of technique, however, is dependent upon sufficient practice of that chord shift. Assigning several songs using those chords gives students some recognition for each bit of practicing that they do.

STARTING

The Bainbridge-Guilford Model is, obviously, not a simple solution to the problem of establishing a meaningful general music program. The implementation of this program is an evolutionary process. There is much to be learned and there are many skills to be acquired if this program is to be successful. The knowledge gained and the development of new teaching techniques, however, provide a new focus and purpose to the teaching of general music. In a program of this design, each music educator may use his or her unique talents, creativity, and artistry.

Sources and Resources

The materials written for the Bainbridge-Guilford Model are available for purchase. This set includes eight different books, a total of 613 pages, written in large print for easy visibility. Sets of materials or individual books are sold to school districts with a limited copy agreement that allows the teacher to make copies needed for instruction within that district.

Inquiries concerning these materials should be sent to:

Traditional Music Materials, 8 Kirby Street Bainbridge, NY 13733

Other materials by Rick Bunting include *Teaching Traditional Music and Instruments: A Classroom Approach* (teaching manual) and *The Dulcimer in the Classroom* (student book and teacher's manual). They are distributed by:

Kendor Music, Main and Grove Streets, PO Box 278, Delevan, New York 14042

A videotape by Rick Bunting, *Recreational Instruments*, published by the State of New York Education Department, is also available. For more information, write:

Bureau of Technology Application, Media Distribution Network, C-7 Concourse Level, Cultural Education Center, Albany, NY 12230

Books and music: There are many books and collections of music that will serve as sources of information or as additional material. The following are suggestions for initial purchase to begin an in-class library. As a teacher spends more time with this program and becomes more familiar with available materials, many other additions will undoubtedly be made to this beginning list. Oak Publications provides a comprehensive selection of books related to traditional instruments. For a free catalog, write to: Oak Publications, Dept. BA, 33 West Sixtieth Street, New York, NY 10023.

Some important additional books are:

Lomax, A. 1960. *The folk songs of North America*. Garden City, NY: Doubleday. A comprehensive source for traditional songs.

O'Neill, F. 1976. *O'Neill's music of Ireland*, revised by Miles Krassen. New York: Oak Publications. A good source for traditional songs.

Wigginton, E., ed. N.d. *Foxfire Books* (Numbers 3, 4, and 6) Garden City, NY: Anchor Books. These books are a good reference for oral journalism activities, and they contain some interesting information on homemade instruments.

Materials

For information about cardboard dulcimer kits, write Backyard Music, PO Box 9047, New Haven, CT 06532.

Records

There are thousands of recordings of traditional music available. Some useful examples include:

Banish Misfortune. June Appal 016.

Dueling Banjos. Warner Brothers 2683.

The Essential Doc Watson. Vanguard 45/46. Guitar.

Feadoga Stain. Shanachie 79006. Pennywhistle.

The Harmonica According to.... Kicking Mule 305.

The Mountain Dulcimer Instrumental Album. Folkways 3570.

Skaggs and Rice. Sugar Hill 3711. Mandolin.

Traditional Tunes. Front Hall 08. Small pipes/concertina.

The View from Home. Flying Fish 037. Autoharp.

Where Did You Get That Hat? Rounder 0172. Clawhammer banjo.

One source for recordings is Elderly Instruments, 1100 North Washington, PO Box 14210, Lansing, MI 48901.

Part Three
FOCUS ON COMPOSITION

Goals and Rationale: The goal of the course is to provide opportunities for senior high school students to develop special music interests and abilities, lifelong learning and involvement in the fine arts, creative achievement and progress leading to feelings of self-worth and self-assurance, and cooperative attitudes in learning to work with others.

Commercial Music provides an alternative to regularly offered music courses for students who want "hands-on" experience in music but lack the skill or interest to participate in performing organizations.

Program Requirements: The following equipment would be adequate to supply three lab stations for a class of 20–22 students: two Yamaha DX-7 II synthesizers, one Yamaha DX-7 synthesizer, one Yamaha QX-21 synthesizer, two Yamaha TX-7 tone generators, one Yamaha RX-11 drum machine, one Yamaha RX-15 drum machine, one Macintosh Plus computer with external drive and Mark of the Unicorn Professional Composer/Performer software, one Yamaha QX-21 sequencer, one Fostex E-8 eight-track recorder, one Fostex 450 mixing console, and one Midiflex reverb unit.

Lab Station 1 is used as the main lab; stations 2 and 3 allow students to learn basic operations of synthesis and sequencing. The approximate cost of equipment for these labs is $12,000–$15,000. Ideally, the three labs should be housed in separate rooms, preferably practice rooms, within the music area. If additional rooms are not available, the labs could be set up in one large room and be outfitted with sufficient headsets for students to work without disturbing other groups.

CHAPTER 6

Commercial Music

by Austin Buffum

Capistrano Valley High School is located in Capistrano, California, an upper-middle-class suburban community. The Capistrano Unified School District encompasses approximately 194 square miles in the southernmost portion of Orange County. A full-time music coordinator and thirty-six music teachers provide instruction for the 23,500 students enrolled in grades K–12. The school district offers a comprehensive elementary music program and secondary programs in band, choir, and orchestra, as well as Commercial Music. The secondary performing groups have distinguished themselves annually at contests, festivals, parades, and field show competitions.

COURSE PHILOSOPHY

In 1983 the California Legislature enacted Senate Bill 813, which reinstituted statewide high school graduation requirements, including one year of either a visual or performing art or a foreign language. The legislation stipulates that art courses should be available to all students, not just to those with special interests in the arts. The bill also recommends that art courses involve student participation, emphasize higher-order thinking skills, and allow students to complete the requirement by taking performance or portfolio courses rather than survey courses that do not include actual participation in visual and performing arts activities.

In 1986, the Capistrano Unified School District initiated the Commercial Music course at Capistrano Valley High School to meet the legislative mandate. The course provides an

CONTACT: *Austin Buffum, district music coordinator, Capistrano Unified School District, 32972 Calle Perfecto, San Juan Capistrano, CA 92675.*

alternative to the regularly offered traditional music courses, yet allows students hands-on opportunities to make music. The structured curriculum provides opportunities for students to develop musical skills and understanding through a contemporary performance medium—electronic technology.

Commercial Music, a two-semester course that meets for fifty-two minutes a day, is open to students in grades 9–12. Instruction is designed to help students acquire basic skills in keyboard, music theory, ear training, and use of electronic equipment. Attention is given to those music skills, concepts, and techniques required of all music classes by the district's music curriculum guide. Also, instruction time is devoted to a unit on sound reinforcement, providing the necessary skills for students to serve the school and the student body as sound technicians for campus events. The goals of this course are to develop special music interests and abilities, lifelong learning and involvement in the fine arts, creative student achievement and progress leading to feelings of self-worth and self-assurance, and cooperative attitudes in learning to work with others. During the first semester, students complete projects and assignments designed to help them acquire skills in using the equipment. Much of the instruction is individualized, allowing individuals or small groups of students to progress through the material at their own pace. A semester project—usually an original composition—is required. Students who elect a second semester of Commercial Music are given special assignments and projects for individual work.

Commercial Music has become a very popular elective in our district. Capistrano Valley High School plans to offer two sections of the course, and two other high schools in the district offer similar courses. Commercial Music is also included in the junior high school curriculum. Two sets of equipment rotate among each of the four junior high schools. Plans are to provide similar experiences at the elementary level.

One of the unexpected benefits of Commercial Music is that many students who complete the course continue music study by electing to participate in one of the school's performing groups; also, the course opens up the music department to an entirely new constituency comprising students who would not otherwise have elected music. I believe that Commercial Music has both strengthened the high school music program and increased enrollment in music.

COMMERCIAL MUSIC CURRICULUM

Initially, all students involved in Commercial Music were given a three-week "crash" course in music theory and ear training. This introduction to theory was taught in a traditional lecture-demonstration mode in the regular band room. We are now convinced that this part of the course will eventually be taught through tutorial software. Some students also required additional practice at a keyboard to acquire basic skills. They were assigned to work on pianos scattered throughout the music facility and were given traditional piano method books so that they could master enough skills to work effectively on the synthesizers.

The foundation curriculum for Commercial Music is designed to develop aesthetic perception, creative expression, skills, historical and cultural awareness, and responsible citizenship and social participation among the students. According to the district's music curriculum guide, students are taught about the following topics:

Drum machine programming: Students grow to understand the basic formats of modern music. They learn basic drum techniques and learn to use the feature in the drum machine sequencer that allows automatic correcting of time errors. Finally, they combine small drum segments into a completed drum sequence (song) using the drum machine.

Frequency modulation synthesis: First, students experiment with the preset sounds on the FM digital synthesizer (using the Yamaha DX-7). They learn to control basic signal parameters on the synthesizer, to use the pitch-bend and modulation wheels, and to control tuning. They also learn about OMNI and mono modes of operation. The students then program or alter the device's synthesis algorithms to create new sounds.

Sequencing: In this part of the course, students learn about MIDI (Musical Instruments Digital Interface) connections, including the in, out, and thru functions. They learn to set the send and receive MIDI channels on the equipment to 1–16 or OMNI and to understand the external sequencer start and stop commands that control the drum machine. They gain a comprehension of real-time digital information recording, learning how to "punch in" and "punch out" and how to "bounce" tracks of recorded information. Finally, they learn about the concepts of step-time recording and automatic correcting.

Multitrack recording: The students learn about the mixing console, learning to control input, trim, and equalization, about how to use bus (signal flow) systems, and about the functions and control of outboard equipment (in this case, a reverberation unit). They learn about multitrack tape deck operations, including threading tape, head cleaning, and punching in and out. The students experience the process of mastering (mixing down) a recording, including equalizing, visual imaging through pan and effects, controlling standard amplitude levels, and developing creativity and uniqueness in the product.

Sound reinforcement: The students learn the basic theory of sound amplification. They analyze and identify the differences in microphone construction and design and demonstrate proper application of this equipment to different situations. The students learn the purpose of the mixing board controls, including pan and equalization controls and monitor and special effect sends, and demonstrate their understanding through application. They evaluate speaker construction, design, and placement, with attention to such common problems as feedback.

The students also gain and demonstrate skills, including *creative skills* (they create original music controlled through the synthesizer and recorded on multitrack equipment), *critical thinking skills* (they manipulate electronic equipment in a creative manner), and *industrial skills* (they demonstrate basic knowledge of the skills currently used in the commercial music industry).

The students are involved in the following dimensions of social participation: They develop respect for their unique abilities and for those of others, they demonstrate the qualities of good citizenship and responsibility in the care of all equipment and materials, and each student uses his or her school and community as a place to apply what has been learned and as a place for continued learning.

COURSE SYLLABUS— FIRST-SEMESTER OVERVIEW

In this course the following units are covered: development of keyboard skills, music theory and harmony, basics of melodic construction and composition, use of keyboard synthesizers, use of sequencers and computers in storing music, creating and editing of sounds on synthesizers, and drum machine programming. Multitrack recording is also covered, and attention is especially given to those skills, concepts, and techniques mentioned in the district music curriculum guide. Each student prepares a semester project (usually an original composition) that is entered into the computer through a synthesizer and is printed by the computer in score form. Students wishing to continue for a second semester are given special assignments and projects for individual work. The following is an outline of lesson plans for the course:

Week 1: introduction to keyboard skills—scales and finger exercises; introduction to music theory—notes and other musical symbols; synthesizer vocabulary—buttons to push

Week 2: keyboard skills—more exercises for finger independence; theory—rhythmic notation; synthesizers—cords, plugs, MIDI functions; composition—elements of music

Week 3: keyboard skills—work with hands together; theory—the overtone series and its importance in synthesizing sound; drum machine vocabulary—buttons to push

Week 4: keyboard skills—more hands-together work, rhythmic independence between hands; harmony—major, minor, diminished, and augmented triads; drum machine—creating patterns using "read-write"

Week 5: keyboard skills—finding and playing triads; theory—writing key signatures and scales; drum machine—creating patterns using "step-write"

Week 6: drum machine—organizing patterns into a song, putting the drum machine in sync with the synthesizer; review and catch-up on all the above concepts, techniques, and skills

Week 7: continued review and preparation for midterm exam; midterm examination 1—keyboard skills test, drum machine test, written test on theory

Week 8: sequencer vocabulary—buttons to push; theory—the Greek modes; composing a song on the drum machine

Week 9: sequencer—storing tracks in the sequencer; continued work on keyboard skills; harmony—seventh chords (major, minor, dominant, diminished, half-diminished)

Week 10: continued work on keyboard skills—finding and playing seventh chords; sequencer—bouncing tracks, erasing, other sequencer functions; theory—inversions of triads, voice-leading

Week 11: continued work on keyboard skills; theory—inversions of seventh chords; synthesizers—editing sounds, sine wave alterations

Week 12: review and catch-up on all topics

Week 13: continued review and preparation for second midterm; midterm examination 2—written theory test, performance test on synthesizer and sequencer

Week 14: synthesizer—more editing (including editing of envelope decay, attack, and release); harmony—diatonic chords in a key and their functions; continued keyboard work; beginning of plans for the semester project

Week 15: computer—using the computer and Performer software to store songs; work on semester project; harmony—cadences and harmonic patterns

Week 16: composition—writing a melody; computer—using the Composer software to print songs; work on semester project

Week 17: composition—harmonizing a melody; compositional devices (such as motifs and formal development); work on semester project

Weeks 18 and 19: work on semester project, which is the final exam; review of above topics, especially as they relate to semester projects

The theory tests listed in the syllabus include questions relating to spelling and identifying chords, identifying and writing intervals and rhythms (by ear), defining important terms, and identifying the functions of various MIDI instruments used in the lab.

SAMPLE LESSON PLANS

Basic Synthesis: Creating Sound With Voltage (non-acoustic instruments)
There are three basic methods for creating sound that are covered in this course:
- Subtractive analog synthesis: A sound is generated by an oscillator (electronic device that sets an electronic vibration by voltage), and then shaped through a series of filters to achieve the final sound. This tends to leave a number of unwanted frequencies or can give a very warm sound (that is, it generates strong voices).
- Additive synthesis: This involves using two sounds (set up as in subtractive analog synthesis) and mixing them as an audio mixer would.
- Digital FM synthesis: In frequency modulation synthesis, the system patented by Yamaha and used on their equipment, a digital (number system) computer calculates by a "what if" method. A "what if" oscillator (not a physical oscillator like those used in analog systems, but a computer that generates numbers that represent the theoretical output of an oscillator) is pushed into, or "modulates," another such oscillator. The ratio of frequencies between the two (or ratios among the multiple) oscillators used in this manner may be controlled. The synthesizer's computer then converts the digital information to an audio signal. Using this method, a very clean sound can be created from scratch.
- Sampling: A computer reads the frequencies read in from a microphone or audio signal, converts them to a digital data string for storage and manipulation, and recreates that sound as an analog (audio) signal on demand.

Basic terms: frequency—pitch (Hz); amplitude—volume.

Voice Initialization
How do you want the sound to start? How hard should it hit and back off? How long should it last after key is released? These are taken care of by the Envelope Generator within each operator.

Step 1. Find the "envelope generator select" control. You will need to set the rates and levels. The basic controls for most synthesizers are A (Attack), D (Decay), S (Sustain), and R (Release). Rates tell how quickly the sound gets to a set level (setting this to zero causes the change in level to occur over a very long time; setting it to ninety-nine produces an immediate change). Level settings tell how loud the sound is when the envelope reaches that point (a setting of zero produces no intensity; ninety-nine is the highest intensity possible).

Step 2. Try various envelope settings. On the DX-7, move the cursor over to R4 (Release/Decay) and reduce the number. What happens when you release the key? Move back to R1 or A. Reduce this value and note the change in the time it takes for the sound to come in.

Step 3. Try to create a realistic bell sound. How big are you going to make it? What would it sound like?

Advanced: Select a sound (instrument) and try to duplicate it.

MATERIALS

The following reference materials are optional:
1. *The Complete DX7*, by Howard Massey (Amsco Publications)
2. *Contemporary Keyboard Magazine* (GPI Publications)
3. *Understanding MIDI*, Jock Baird (Ed.) (Amsco Publications)
4. *Synthesizer Basics, Vols. I and II—Keyboard*, Synthesizer Library (Hal Leonard Pub.)
5. *The Original DX7 Patch Fake Book, Vol. I*, compiled by Lorenz Rychner and S. Frankfurt (Alexander Pub.)

These materials can be ordered through your local music store or through the school from a local vendor. They are excellent references for the class and for future needs.

ENROLLMENT AND IMPLEMENTATION

Because of the limitations imposed by the availability of equipment, we try to limit enrollment to twenty students. Initially, twenty-two students were enrolled in the pilot class at Capistrano Valley High School. Of these, ten had never enrolled in a traditional instrumental or choral music class offered at the school. There was no need to advertise or recruit for the class—students had heard of the program through "word of mouth," and the class was easily filled. Following the pilot program, Commercial Music was implemented as a one-year elective in the visual and performing arts at all three of the district's high schools.

Not all music teachers were receptive to or confident about the prospect of teaching such a class; consequently, the positive aspects of the program were stressed, especially the idea of opening up the music department to an entirely new constituency. After working with this program for several years, I believe that Commercial Music can only strengthen and enlarge existing high school music programs.

Another important aspect of implementation is the need for sufficient in-service training prior to teaching the class. In retrospect, we could have done more in this regard to make the initial offerings at the two new campuses more effective. With the demands of an active music program, time for learning a new technology such as that involved with Commercial Music is limited. Our plan involved using the original teacher from Capistrano Valley High School, Lynn Olinger, as a mentor teacher. As part of a formalized mentor program in our district, Lynn was able to work with these teachers at his facility to teach about the technology and to assist in the installation at the new location. With helpful insights based on his use of the equipment, Lynn visited each teacher several times to observe the class in action and to make suggestions.

Security: This was an obvious area of concern from the beginning of the pilot program. Each piece of equipment was separately attached to lock-down pads such as those used on computers. After all equipment was secured to the table tops, each table was bolted into a wall. Also, heat-sensing alarm systems were added at each site. All equipment is removed from the labs during the summer recess and the winter and spring holidays and is brought to a secure location at the education center. We have experienced no losses of equipment.

Current considerations: Enrollments in this course have continued to grow, and we currently plan to offer two periods of Commercial Music at Capistrano Valley High School. Current enrollment at Capistrano Valley is thirty-five, which is really too large for a class of this nature. The three labs at Capistrano Valley have been expanded to include twelve work stations.

JUNIOR HIGH APPLICATIONS

With the implementation of Commercial Music at each of our three high schools, we began to look at how this technology could be introduced at the junior high and elementary levels. In our district, the junior high school is structured for grades 7–8. The school day for seventh grade students consists of six periods, including only one elective choice. If students are not enrolled in a vocal or instrumental music class, they usually take a survey course, Fine and Practical Arts, as their elective. This course consists of a nine-week introduction to visual arts, industrial arts, foods and fabrics, and music. It had been observed that although the first three areas of the course involved students in numerous hands-on activities, the music portion of the class seemed all too often to find students listening to and learning about but seldom actively "doing" music. This seemed like the natural place in the junior high school curriculum to introduce MIDI technology.

Two sets of equipment were purchased to rotate among each of our four junior high schools, each set consisting of sixteen Yamaha DX-100 synthesizers, one Yamaha DX-27 synthesizer, one Yamaha QX-21 synthesizer, one Yamaha RX-17 drum machine, one Roland CK-60 keyboard amplifier, and four Boss B-800 mixers.

Since students rotate in and out of the music portion of Fine and Practical Arts every nine weeks, this set of equipment is made available to each school for a 4 1/2 -week unit. Students are introduced to basic theory and keyboard skills in a class setting, usually two students to each DX-100 synthesizer. After exploring the sounds and creating a "sound composition," students are expected to create their own piece of music as a final project. As they complete this project working at the DX-100, they are able to come to the front of the room and sequence their composition using the DX-27, QX-21, and RX-17 units. With help from the teacher, most are able to complete this step, after which compositions are "mixed down" onto a cassette tape. Students are then able to take home with them the piece they "made" in music class, in the same way they are able to take home projects made in visual arts, industrial arts, and foods and fabrics.

Students are also made aware of the commercial music opportunities available at each high school, and many are now expressing a desire to further their introduction to MIDI technology by enrolling in the course at the high school level. Also, the music portion of Fine and Practical Arts has become the most popular in the rotation. Teachers feel that this has been accomplished through the introduction of MIDI technology, and they have noted the improved feeling toward the music program in general at each junior high school.

PROGRAM BENEFITS

There are many objections music educators can have about a program using MIDI technology. However, many of those resistant in the beginning have begun to see the benefits to their overall music program. Enrollments have grown in traditional music classes, which have benefited from this "opening up" to a new segment of the school population. Even those students not currently enrolled in a music class will acknowledge—based on their observations of this attempt to include new technology in our music curriculum—that we have a good program.

Music teachers have also observed the application of Commercial Music to the teaching of traditional music classes. High school orchestra students use a sequenced version of the annual spring musical to practice their parts. Unlike a tape recording, a sequenced version can be played at any tempo without altering the pitch. Students can gain confidence with these often difficult parts through practice at progressively faster tempos. Rewinding to the beginning of a song or entire work may take just a few seconds instead of minutes. Of course, once entered into a sequencing program such as Professional Composer/Performer, it is a simple matter to transpose parts to an "easier" key and print hard copies.

Using the lab's eight-track recording equipment, school groups that need to submit demonstration tapes can make and mix down tapes of excellent quality, again under the guidance of Commercial Music students. With appropriate copyright permission, high school show choirs can "commission" their own arrangements, complete with drum tracks, rather than being limited to those selections commercially available with background tracks. These are only a few of the many possible applications of this technology to the teaching of "regular" music classes.

Administrators support Commercial Music for several reasons. First, it strengthens enrollments and provides new scheduling options. Second, it integrates music teachers and music curricula with technology and other areas of the curriculum. We now see science and mathematics teachers expressing interest in what the music department is doing. English, drama, and social science teachers have requested that original music be composed for various events or units of study in their own areas. Students from the Commercial Music classes are called on to provide sound reinforcement for various school activities. In the future, we hope to include film scoring as part of this class. Demonstration and instructional videos produced at the school and by the district could include original music produced in the Commercial Music classes.

The district is supportive of Commercial Music because of its innovative use of technology in the arts. Not only have we been able to provide a viable elective offering for the nonperforming high school student, we have also demonstrated that our district is progressive in its use of technology, especially in integrating music with the rest of the high school curriculum.

Goals and Rationale: The overall objective of projects in the "sound" segment of this program is to give students (including those with no previous musical experience) an opportunity to have creative experiences with sound. These experiences give the teacher the opportunity to explore with the students the various properties of music (pitch, rhythm, timbre, and form) in various degrees and applications and give the students the opportunity to understand these properties through hands-on creative activities.

Program Requirements: Computers with software for building sight-singing and rhythm sight-reading skills and other aural and music literacy skills; the Tap Master and PitchMaster systems; electronic keyboards, tape recorder and microphones; video camera.

CHAPTER 7

Creative Arts Camp

by Christine D. Hermanson

T he Creative Arts Camp is a summer activity of the Sarasota Fine Arts Academy, a private music and art school in Sarasota, Florida. Each camp session is a week-long, self-contained unit consisting of five 3½-hour sessions. Many campers elect to attend a second week to do the same projects again with new ideas and to try for results polished by greater experience.

Each daily camp session is split into three one-hour segments: sound, visual arts and crafts, and musicianship. The musicianship segment takes place in the master musician computer lab, where students (with and without prior music experience) work on building sight-singing and rhythm sight-reading skills, and other aural and music literacy skills, by using a wide variety of computer software products and the Tap Master and PitchMaster systems.

The overall objective of projects in the "sound" segment of this program is to give students (including those with no previous musical experience) an opportunity to have creative experiences with sound. These experiences give the teacher the opportunity to explore with the students the various properties of music (pitch, rhythm, timbre, and form) in various degrees and applications and give the students the opportunity to understand these properties through hands-on creative activities. The activities described in this chapter were designed to fulfill this objective.

Sound Composition

In this project, students make a sound composition, an activity that helps students discover that music is sound organized in time, and that unity and variety are key elements in a successful musical composition and can be achieved through repetition and contrast, planned dynamic contrasts, and musical form (organization of repetition and contrast).

Material and equipment requirements include a "Blueprint for Sound Composition" form (one for each group of students) and sounds (supplied by the students). In my experience these sounds have ranged from the ordinary (kazoos, mouth-pops, and kitchen pan lids) to the exotic (smashing a light bulb in a metal garbage can). This smashing light bulb provided a climactic ending to a composition and was only allowed once—on the actual recording. Recorded with electronic reverberation, it was very effective. The project also requires a tape recorder. (The more sophisticated the tape recorder, the more sophisticated the outcome. However, very effective results can be obtained with an ordinary cassette recorder.) Options include using (1) a multitrack cassette recorder for layering sounds onto individual tracks, (2) a mixer for direct input of several microphones or microphones and synthesizers (many students have portable synthesizer keyboards with digital sampling capabilities), and (3) a cassette recorder or mixer with reverb or echo features.

Procedures: The project generally takes three or four one-hour class sessions to complete. Students work in groups of four to six; each group is given the "Blueprint for Sound Composition," and each student selects a sound to be used in the composition.

The teacher explains the "blueprint" (see accompanying example). First, each vertical column represents a segment of time. The group determines the length of time (for example, one column could be five seconds, one could be three seconds, and so forth). Second, group members list each sound along the left-hand column in the blanks provided. Next, the group will decide which sound or sounds are to be played in each time segment. Wherever an "instrument" is to be played, students color in the square opposite the instrument and in the correct column. Finally, students can use more than one "blueprint" form to make longer compositions.

As the groups are working (and later, practicing) the teacher asks questions and offers suggestions to help the students understand the purpose of unity and variety, dynamic contrasts, and musical form. These specific musical properties should not be taught as abstractions, but rather as the outgrowth of the development of the sound compositions.

On the second day, students bring sounds and groups practice and make adjustments (edit the projects) in preparation for recording. The compositions are then recorded, and each composition (and possibly the compositions of other groups in other classes) is played back for class discussion and evaluation.

Sounds & Performers	Seconds ❏	❏	❏	❏	❏	❏	❏

Blueprint for sound composition

Radio Commercial

This project is designed to integrate background music, sound effects, and spoken text into a radio commercial. This helps students discover how music and sound effects are used in advertising to catch the attention of the listener and sell the idea or the products and gives the students an opportunity to create their own background music and sound effects.

Material and equipment requirements include "Radio Commercial" forms (one for each pair of students), sound effects (supplied by the students), and two tape recorders—one to play back the background music tape during the final recording and one to record the final product as it comes out of the mixer.

The students also need a mixer that accepts the direct input of several microphones and synthesizers (which are optional but recommended). Radio Shack sells a very inexpensive mixer that allows students to adjust the volumes of the narration, background music, and sound effects to the proper balances. Other options include using a multitrack cassette recorder for layering sounds on individual tracks (this can be used instead of a mixer) and a cassette recorder or mixer with reverb or echo features.

Procedures: This project generally takes up three or four one-hour class sessions. The students work in groups of two to four. Each group is provided with a "Radio Commercial" form (see the accompanying example) that they complete to organize their efforts. The groups select or compose music for the introduction (and background, if appropriate) of their commercials. The background music is recorded on a tape that is separate from the one that will be used to record the final commercial.

Students then select and obtain the sound effects. If "live" sounds or sounds reproduced by a digital sampling keyboard are used for sound effects, the effects should be played live during the final recording to provide exact control of the timing and placement in the final commercial. This avoids the inherent difficulties involved in synchronizing two or more tape decks. Students practice reading the script with the background music and sound effects and then record the final product. Finally, each commercial is played back for class discussion and evaluation. The students are asked if they would buy the featured product based on the advertisement.

Product Name _____
Description _____
List the good points of your product that will help it sell.

_____
_____

Describe the sound effects you will use to help sell your product.

_____
_____

What type of music will best represent your product? (For example, fast, slow, vocal, piano, symphonic, rock/pop, or classical.)

_____
_____

Write your script for the voice track. (You may want to write in the sound effects you will use.)

_____
_____

Radio commercial form

Television Commercial

In this project, the students proceed as with the radio commercial but omit the final tape recorder capabilities and use a video camera for production of the final recording. They must also add the costuming and other visual effects needed for a visual presentation. The accompanying form may help the students organize their work.

Product Name _____
Description _____
List the good points of your product that will help it sell.

_____
_____

Describe the sound effects you will use to help sell your product.

_____
_____

What type of music will best represent your product? (For example, fast, slow, vocal, piano, symphonic, rock/pop, or classical.)

_____
_____

Write your script. Include the sound effects, visual effects, and the costumes (if any) you will use.

_____
_____

Television commercial form

First Improvisation/Composition Project

1. With your right hand pick out any group of five black keys in order. Place your thumb and each finger on each black key. Play the keys up and down in order. Now play the keys in any order. Try holding down the damper pedal and play the keys again in any order.

2. Move to another group of five black keys and play the keys in order (as in step one).

3. Pick another group of five black keys. (There are only five different groups of black keys on the keyboard; the others are repeats of the five groups, either higher or lower.) Which group or groups do you like the best? Pick two groups for your improvisation.

4. Now establish the rhythm pattern for your improvisation. For example, you can use the rhythm pattern to a song most people know: "Mary Had a Little Lamb." Say the words and clap your hands or tap once for every syllable of the words in the song.

/ / / / / / / —   / / /— / / / —
Ma-ry had a lit -tle lamb   Lit-tle lamb, lit -tle lamb

/ / / / / / / /   / / / / /— — —
Ma-ry had a lit-tle lamb its   fleece was white as snow

5. Say the words to the song again, and instead of clapping or tapping, play one of the keys in your group of five black keys for each accent. (Your melody is not supposed to sound like "Mary Had a Little Lamb.") Repeat the song on another set of five black keys. Now, create an ending by repeating the keys you played for the words "fleece was white as snow" three times. For an even better ending, try playing softer at each repeat. Can you think of anything else that would make a good ending?

6. Now you are ready to add a left-hand part. Place the thumb and "pinkie" finger of your left hand over the two black keys in Illustration 1. Now move your fingers down one black key to play the two notes in Illustration 2. Practice playing the keys in Illustration 1, then those in Illustration 2, and then play each illustration alternately.

7. Now try playing with both hands together. (Your right-hand notes might be different every time you play the song—that's okay.) To help you keep your place, whisper the words to the song as you play. Now play the song as you did in step four, adding the ending. Try thinking of another familiar song with a different rhythm.

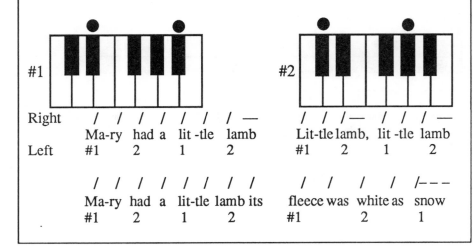

Project instruction sheet for the "First Improvisation/Composition Project"

Story with Sound Effects

In this project, students are asked to create sound effects for use in the narration and audio recording of an original or existing story. This exercise helps students discover how to use a synthesizer in creating and modifying various sound effects. They are given an introduction to wave forms and the effect of changes in the envelope of a sound (the contour that traces the change in "loudness" from the onset of a sound to its final decay), instructed about how and when to use sound to enhance the presentation of a story, and shown how "the professionals" do it.

Material and equipment requirements for the project include either an original story written by the group or an existing story with the inherent potential for illustration with sounds. The students also need sources for such sounds as footsteps, slamming car doors, and bells. Use a synthesizer with preprogrammed sound effects that can be altered or a synthesizer with digital sampling capabilities. It might be possible to borrow a synthesizer from a dealer for a short-term project such as this. This would allow the use of a more sophisticated synthesizer than might be available through the school or the students. (Remind the dealer that this would be good advertising!) Finally, this project requires a cassette recorder—optionally, one that has a mixer with reverb or echo features.

Procedures: Completion of this project generally requires three one-hour class sessions. Students work in groups of four to six. The teacher provides a demonstration of sound effects generated by a synthesizer, such as dog barks, waves, crickets, footsteps, train whistles, and human whistles. Students are shown how these effects can be modified by changing the envelope of each sound.

Students either find or write a story that allows some creative use of sound effects. They may find inspiration for a story from the sound effects available (each group must be given an equal opportunity to use the synthesizer). Finally, the narration of the story, including the sound effects, is recorded and the recordings are played back and evaluated.

First Improvisation/Composition Project

This project is designed to provide students who have little or no keyboard experience with a structure to "make up" their own pieces on the keyboard. This will help them discover (1) that music is sound organized in time; (2) that unity and variety (the key elements in a successful musical composition) can be achieved through repetition and contrast of thematic material, planned dynamic contrast, and musical form (organization of repetition and contrast); and (3) ways to create an effective ending.

Material and equipment requirements for this project include an electronic keyboard with outputs that can be patched into a cassette recorder, a cassette recorder and tapes, and a student instruction sheet that outlines procedures for the project (to enable independent work).

Procedures: This project takes approximately twenty to thirty minutes per student per station. The teacher explains the project, discusses the instruction sheet step by step, and demonstrates an example—the students then work individually. Because this is an individualized project, it is best to have students work in an independent learning center while other class activities are taking place. A keyboard with earphones and a cassette recorder patched in constitutes one learning center.

Students really enjoy creative projects such as the ones outlined here when the projects are structured properly and managed efficiently. In my experience, creative projects are most effective if students are given a structural framework within which to work. Nothing motivates students more than success!

Goals and Rationale: Music Lab offers students opportunities to examine the use of computer music technology as it affects the motion picture, TV, radio, and record industries; to acquire skills in the use of synthesizers, drum machines, audio processing, and recording techniques; to create compositions in various rock and top forty music styles using various computer music systems; and to investigate possible career choices in today's music business.

The state of New York requires every high school student to complete a full year, one-credit course in either Studio Art or Music in Our Lives. According to the state syllabus, Music in Our Lives focuses on music technology and requires hands-on experiences in music that are relevant to the lives of the students. Music Lab, the general music course designed for grades 9–12 at Shoreham-Wading River High School, meets the state requirements.

Program Requirements: Music Lab can be taught successfully with a variety of equipment (chosen from among the continually changing models available from the many manufacturers in this field) that meets any of a variety of budget levels. A studio could be set up with an inexpensive keyboard such as the Casio SK-5, a four-track tape recorder such as the Fostex X-15, and an amplifier such as the Gorilla GB-30. A more elaborate studio might use a sequencer such as the Alesis MT-24 (or a computer with MIDI interface and sequencer software), synthesizers such as the Yamaha DX-100 keyboard and the Alesis HR-16 drum machine, MIDI and audio cables, and an amplifier. Alternately, a studio might use one or more self-contained MIDI workstations such as the Ensoniq SQ-80, the Korg M-1, or the Roland D-20, and high-quality workstations (including samplers) such as the Roland W3 or the Ensoniq EPS.

CHAPTER 8

Music Lab

by Tony Messina

The Shoreham-Wading River School District is located on Long Island, about seventy miles east of New York City. The small, rural school district has a total enrollment of approximately 2,700 students in grades K–12. The high school houses 678 students in grades 9–12. In its first year, approximately 12 percent of the total high school population elected Music Lab.

Music Lab is the outgrowth of my experimentation with musique concrète with middle school students more than fifteen years ago. We collected and displayed items such as old swing sets, waffle irons, and hubcaps in the music room to give it a "cool" environment. These "sculptures" became instruments as we used their unique sounds to accompany student-created poems and short stories. Capitalizing on student interest and motivation, I designed lessons that required students to create music in the style of Varèse and other contemporary composers.

Currently, in the high school course, students work with computers, synthesizers, sequencers, and drum machines. They learn to compose—without first learning eighteenth- and nineteenth-century theory and compositional techniques. Instead of using pencil and manuscript paper, students use a computer with Musical Instrument Digital Interface (MIDI) and sequencer software (the ultimate composing tool), a MIDI drum synthesizer, and one or more MIDI keyboard synthesizers. The sequencer software essentially turns the computer into a digital multitrack tape recorder that can move musical events around just as a word processor moves words.

CONTACT: Tony Messina, Shoreham-Wading River High School, PO Box 337, Shoreham, NY 11786.

THE COMPOSITIONAL PROCESS

Students need no previous musical knowledge to succeed in Music Lab. They create compositions by working on the rhythm, melody, and chord progression separately. They create a rhythm track using the drum machine and sequencer, discovering that rhythms are created with sound and silence. Using the "play," "record," "listen," and "edit" modes of the sequencer, they create rhythmic patterns and learn to extend the patterns by repetition or alteration. The resulting extended rhythm becomes the melodic rhythm of a new tune or composition.

By recording or "saving" different patterns on different tracks, students learn that they can layer their patterns, creating an effect similar to that created by an entire percussion section. These patterns can be played back at a faster or slower speed by adjusting the tempo control.

To these patterns they add a chord progression. They experiment once again by using the "play," "record," "listen," and "edit" modes of the sequencer, and "save" the desired progression. Later, students "cut and paste" these events into a wide variety of compositions, and add spoken or sung texts.

MUSIC JOURNALS

In addition to composing and experimenting with sounds, students keep music journals—notebooks in which they write music (using both traditional and nontraditional notation) and record their reactions to music. The journal serves as a notebook, a workbook, a log, and a personal diary. By keeping a journal, students are encouraged to think about what they've learned and give more thought to the organization of their compositions. We begin the year with the agreement that I will read the journals from time to time and make comments on them.

Students are encouraged to daydream in their journals: I explain that daydreaming is referred to as "research and development" in business, and in science it's called "hypothesizing." Periodicals and other publications on music and related technology are available for the students in the Music Lab. These publications provide technical information and keep everyone—students and teacher alike—aware of recent developments in hardware and software.

COURSE OUTLINE

We consider the questions "What are computers?" and "What is computer music?"

History: We discuss electronic music and today's technology, starting with the musique concrète of Pierre Henri, Pierre Schaeffer, Edgard Varèse, and John Cage. I introduce technical considerations, such as monophonic and polyphonic synthesizers, presets, microprocessors, integrated systems for computer generated sound, and MIDI.

Active computer music systems: This discussion includes an introduction to the concepts of note information, interfaces, sequencers and digital recording, voice librarians, and digital sound design and sound reconstruction.

Interactive computer music: I introduce the students to the ideas of sampling, sequencing and sequencer software, disk storage, sampling and editing, and MIDI clocks and synchronization modes.

Fundamentals: In addition to a section on designing a MIDI studio environment and one on living American composers, I introduce the students to rhythm (including standard and altered notations and improvisation); melody (patterns and phrases, modes, and key centers); and harmony (building chords, chord progressions, and tone clusters). We discuss form (its uses and misuses and the problem of developing a style) and lyrics (general principles such as identifying what one wants to say and developing a story line as well as specifics for the course, such as what we can and cannot use in school). Finally, we discuss songwriting (putting it all together and how to be your own editor).

SAMPLE LESSONS

During the school year, I do a great deal of work with groups of three or four students, having them work together on a variety of projects. These groups are involved every day with planning, playing, rehearsing, listening, analyzing, and synthesizing. I construct the groups so that any one student could be the composer, the computer operator, the singer, the keyboard player, the drum machine programmer, or the visual artist for a performance. The students share the writings from their journals as well.

Music Lab is different from most general music programs because I have cut loose the "general music" frame of mind. In teaching, I often modify the original lesson to provide the students with a positive learning experience. The product of the course is a wide variety of *original* compositions, written and performed by students who represent the entire student population—not just a chosen few. The course more closely approximates the conservatory model for teaching composition, but uses variants such as graphic and altered notation, tone clusters, and abstract harmonies. It uses real-time improvisational methods (facilitated by the computer) rather than classical theory-based composition.

The Pledge, Part 1

This lesson attempts to engage students in a dialogue about patriotism and nationalism, to have them define collectively a moral point of view with regard to what the words of the "Pledge of Allegiance to the Flag" really mean. In the process, they compose and play an original piece of computer music and receive an introduction to digital sampling (of the voice only).

The lesson's methodology is directed at the development of reflective thinking, analysis, the construction of knowledge, and inquiry (creating a disequilibrium and then resolving the discrepancies related to the flag and the Pledge). I focus on the idea of a point of view, supporting the student's view and assisting the students in understanding other points of view and the presence of multiple frames of reference.

Resources required:
- Computer (such as an Apple Macintosh)
- Printer (such as an Imagewriter II)
- Sequencer software (such as Midi Mac by Opcode)
- Word processing software (such as Microsoft Word)
- Music writing software (such as Music Writer by Passport Design)
- Graphics software (such as Dazzel Draw or MacPaint)
- Digital sampler (such as the Ensoniq EPS keyboard)
- MIDI-capable synthesizer (such as the Casio CZ-1)

Assignment: Students are asked to compose an electronic and computer music sound track to accompany the "Pledge of Allegiance to the Flag." They are required to use the Pledge as we know it, and also to use a variation of the Pledge ("cutting and pasting" on the word processor) using only the original words. The music itself must use three to five words, which are sampled by the computer.

The students are asked to use at least one line (melody), at least two chords, and no drum track. They are asked to develop a counterpoint to the vocal lines of the original Pledge, the Pledge variation, and the sampled version of the Pledge. They are required to say the original Pledge at least once during the piece; they must then redesign the Pledge (form a variation) using the original words to form a second Pledge that is spoken or sung in harmony.

After examining the Pledge, I ask each student to use computer graphics to draw a flag that represents how he or she feels about America. Alternately, I ask them to draw a logo, a badge, a hat, or a symbol of some kind that may represent America.

Teaching sequence: As preparation, we play roles (I take the part of a recent immigrant to the United States who knows nothing about the Pledge). We also have discussions on the flag, asking: What does the Pledge stand for? What do the words mean? Why do we pledge to the flag? Do people demonstrate patriotism by saying the Pledge? What does it mean to be patriotic? Is it important to be patriotic? Why? Who said so? Are those people right?

Then, slowly, and one at a time, we examine, define, and try to understand the words of the Pledge. The teacher can stimulate the students' thought by asking questions such as "Why do you feel that way? Who else can understand what you have just said? Why is that important?"

The lesson takes four to five class periods. Of these, one is spent in discussion. In the second, students write, plan, and start rehearsing their compositions. They do this in groups of two to four students, one group at a time. Rehearsing and recording the Pledge occurs during one or two class periods; generating computer graphics accounts for the last class.

The Pledge, Part 2

In this lesson, the students explore the possibility of a perfect society and investigate its characteristics. They then write a "Pledge of Allegiance" for this new society.

Resources required:
- Computer (such as an Apple Macintosh)
- Printer (such as an Imagewriter II)
- Sequencer software (such as Midi Mac by Opcode)
- Word processing software (such as Microsoft Word)
- Music writing software (such as Music Writer by Passport Design)
- Graphics software (such as Dazzel Draw or MacPaint)
- Digital sampler (such as the Ensoniq EPS keyboard)
- MIDI-capable synthesizer (such as the Casio CZ-1)

Assignment: The students are directed to write new Pledges for their hypothetical societies and compose computer-music sound tracks for their Pledges. For this project, I require them to use digital sampling in producing their sound tracks. The students are asked to use at least two melody lines, a four-chord harmonic progression, a drum track, and a single vocal line (with no counterpoint). I ask them to draw, using computer graphics, a flag to go with their new Pledges and to draw maps of their hypothetical countries.

Teaching sequence: We start by working with some of the same ideas that were used in the "Pledge, Part 1" lesson. I then ask the students to imagine what a perfect society would be like and what things would be important in that society. The lesson takes six to seven class periods. The first one or two periods are spent planning the new Pledge, three are used for planning and recording the student compositions, and two are used for producing computer graphics.

Understanding the relationship between a note value and how it relates to a particular meter, as many music educators will surely agree, is a difficult concept for many students to grasp. In an effort to maximize our teaching time, I suggest that a modification of the standard notation system be examined.

Notation

In this lesson, which takes three to six class periods, we discuss the correlation between symbols and objects in the real world. I use the examples of the alphabet, road signs, expressions such as Pepsi's "Catch the Wave" and Dodge's "Ram Tough," and the symbol of loyalty involved in saluting the flag. We discuss the manner in which symbols are really rules that people agree on. I explain how music notation is a system of rules and ask each student to make up an original system of music notation. We compare the resulting systems, looking for similarities among the newly invented notations.

Resources required:
- Objects for "found sounds"

Teaching sequence: I introduce a "Play/Rest" system. This is based on the fact that the two most basic events in music are play and rest. I begin introducing the students to this system with four-beat patterns, using quarter notes and quarter rests; these are the easiest units to understand because of their one-to-one correspondence to the beats in a simple $\frac{4}{4}$ pattern. I use a slash (/) to represent a played beat, and a zero ("0") to represent a rest. A string of four-beat patterns (avoiding the concept of $\frac{4}{4}$) might then be as follows:

$$\|: / / / 0 - / / / / - 0 / / / - / / / 0 - / / / / :\|$$

I have the class write and play rhythms using this devised notation system. We start with a simple, single rhythm pattern, and I stress to the students that songs are made up of patterns that connect to form sections that are in turn chained together to form the entire piece.

I define tempo as a steady pulse (using a metronome, clapping my hands, or snapping my fingers). I start a steady pulse by saying "one, two, ready, play," and ask the students to play a given rhythm on their desktops. I then have the students write rhythms to be played on "found objects" (such as hubcaps and chunks of wood or metal), drums, or synthesizers. Next, I ask the students to write pieces by chaining patterns together. Finally, the students are ready to develop patterns that use eight-beat units (played twice as fast), alternating them with their established four-beat patterns to produce eighth-note rhythms.

Recording Rhythms on a Sequencer

Resources required:
- Sequencer (or computer with sequencer software)
- Amplifier and patch cords

Teaching sequence: I start this lesson, which takes three to five class periods, with a basic overview of "how to use the sequencer" from the unit's manual. We then record a bass (or "kick") drum track on track one, using a simple four-measure pattern such as

$$|: / / / / - / / / 0 :|$$

I then ask the students to try a four-measure pattern, using eighth notes, and to experiment with different tracks. They save the track they like best to the memory or disk drive. Following the sequencer manual, I then explain editing and introduce "quantizing" (the process by which a computer can correct minor deviations from correct rhythm).

The students then add the snare drum on the second and fourth beats:

$$|: / 0 / 0 - 0 / 0 / :|$$

They quantize the tracks they have produced (if needed), experiment with different snare tracks, and save the best of their efforts.

I introduce the idea of polyrhythm by showing the students how to "layer" drum tracks. I show them the following symbolic representation:

Player #1 or kick drum

$$|: / / / / - / / / 0 :|$$

Player #2 or snare drum

$$|: 0 / 0 / - 0 / 0 / :|$$

Player #3 or cymbals (a sixteen-beat pattern)

$$|: / / / 0 - / / / / - 0 / / / - 0 / / / :|$$

Player #4 or cowbell (a sixteen-beat pattern)

$$|: 0 0 / / - 0 0 / / - 0 / / 0 - 0 / / 0 :|$$

The students record the cymbal and cowbell tracks, and save the drum tracks as "Sequence 1." They repeat the entire procedure and learn to chain sequences together to form a song.

A good drum song could take up all of the tracks in the sequencer (often, only eight tracks are available), leaving no room to record a bass line, chords, or solos. I teach the students to conserve memory space by collaborating in playing more than one instrument on a single track: as they are working in groups of two to four, one can play the kick drum, one can play the snare, and so forth. Of course, a single player could play all of the drum parts, just as a piano player plays more than one note at a time. Two or more fingers playing drum tracks at the same time takes some practice, but this technique is commonly used in the recording industry to "lay down" drum tracks.

I then talk about ABA form and its use in pop music as verse-chorus-solo. I play some pop records and chart the form. We follow with student performances of some of their rhythm songs, and I use open-ended questioning to discuss the students pieces, asking: Why did you use those rhythms? What do you like most about your rhythm song? I also play students' pieces for other classes for analysis.

Chords

Harmonic theory as an abstract concept is difficult for many students to understand. I have had success, on the other hand, in having students add chord progressions to drum tracks that they have created. This approach is far easier to understand than two-dimensional writing of harmonies on the chalkboard. Students want to *do* it; they do not want to talk about doing it. To know music is to play music. A real-time computer music workstation where kids can play, record, listen to, and edit musical ideas is a motivational and musical tool.

Resources required:
- Keyboard (synthesizer)
- Sequencer (or computer with sequencer software)
- Amplifier and patch cords

Teaching sequence: I begin this lesson by having the students take a graphic look at the keyboard. I draw pictures and explain the system of grouping two and three black keys. In the key of C major, I then show them how to make chords (defined as two or more notes struck at the same time). I ask the students to experiment with lots of combinations of white keys to determine whether some chords sound better than others and to identify which chords they prefer. We then try to come up with a theory or a set of rules for chords. Through this process I teach in terms of open and close spacing rather than consonant and dissonant intervals. The students then develop chord books with graphic chord charts, and write two-chord progressions (using chords from their books).

Finally, I demonstrate chord progressions (using Dm7 and Em7) in relation to a drum track. I walk the class through a twelve-measure piece with drums, bass, and chords. The students share ideas and critique the process of finding a "good" chord progression (defined here as two or more chords played in a pattern along with a rhythm pattern).

Goals and Rationale: The goal of the program is to provide an environment and experiences whereby students can explore and experiment with sound in meaningful ways. Students are assisted in developing proficiency with electronic equipment, producing original projects, notating music, listening intelligently to music, developing and using a music vocabulary, understanding the evolving culture of the twenty-first century, and becoming familiar with the role music has played and continues to play in society.

Program Requirements: A tape deck, a mixer, a sequencer, a MIDI-capable keyboard synthesizer, a drum synthesizer, and a computer with MIDI interface and sequencing software; books, magazines, filmstrips, videos, recordings, and films for inspiration and stimulation of creativity and for discussion.

CHAPTER 9

Music Technology

by Anne D. Modugno

The Greenwich High School graduation requirement in the arts is four points (equivalent to one Carnegie unit), of which two must be in the visual and performing arts and two in either the visual and performing arts or in the applied arts (business, home economics, and industrial arts). Students must amass eighty points to graduate.

Our "Course of Study Guide" mandates that two points of the arts requirement be satisfied by taking courses in the departments of art, theater arts, media, or music. These four departments offer fifty-five courses giving each student a variety of options in terms of developing and expressing his or her artistic potential. Beyond fulfilling the graduation requirement, many students elect additional courses in the arts to further broaden their educational background, to pursue an area of specific interest, or to prepare for a career or for college.

THE SCHOOL AND THE CURRICULUM

Greenwich High School has six periods a day in a seven-day schedule. Courses in the arts have been flexibly scheduled, providing access to all students. All of the performing groups and many of the students in the general music program come to music class for three periods, or "blocks," out of the seven-day cycle. This is in contrast to academic courses, which meet for six blocks during the seven-day cycle. Most students attend five of these academic courses—this gives them a limited amount of open time in their schedules. Scheduling a course for three days out of the seven-day cycle allows interested music students to sign up for both the instrumental and vocal music programs as well as for the general music program. Sixteen percent of the student body participates in the music program.

Creating and developing a curriculum is similar to creating and developing a musical composition. As the composer must make choices for combining sounds into the many possibilities of forms and tonal systems to create a well-balanced musical composition, the curriculum writer must make choices from a wide range of musical experiences to structure a well-balanced music curriculum for all students.

CONTACT: Anne D. Modugno, 126 Hunting Ridge Road, Stamford, CT 06903.

PHILOSOPHY OF THE MUSIC DEPARTMENT

No culture exists without some form of musical expression. Every society's aesthetic needs have been documented by anthropologists and psychologists; this human character is also evident in the sheer number of musical works all over the world. Music, along with all the arts, has a fundamental place in a person's complete education. Music is recognized universally as an essential element in the full education program.

The Greenwich High School music faculty believe that music as an aesthetic experience is significant in everyone's life. Music challenges teachers' creative and innovative skills and puts them in the position of learners. It is a subject that lends itself to a teacher-student relationship for learning, experimenting with, and experiencing new musical ideas. High-quality work is encouraged and rewarded.

COURSE OFFERINGS

The music program offers a wide variety of subjects for all students. The only groups for which students must audition in grades 9–12 are chamber singers, orchestra (except for string players, who need not audition), and jazz ensemble. All other courses are open to students with or without a musical background.

Performance Ensembles
- Band: Meets for the full year, 3 blocks; 2 points
- Chamber Singers: Full year, 3 blocks; 2 points
- Color Guard: Meets an undetermined number of blocks during the first and fourth grading periods; 1 point
- Concert Choir: Full year, 3 blocks; 2 points
- Freshman Chorus: Full year, 3 blocks; 2 points
- Girls' Chorus: Full year, 3 blocks; 2 points
- Guitar: Full year, 3 blocks; 2 points—may also be taken for the first or second semester, 6 blocks; 2 points
- Instrumental Class: Scheduled for the first or second semester, 1 block; 1 point
- Jazz Band: Full year, 3 blocks; 2 points
- Jazz Choir: Full year, 3 blocks; 2 points
- Jazz Ensemble: Full year, meetings to be assigned; 2 points
- String Ensemble: Full year, 1 block; 1 point
- String Quartet: Full year, 1 block; 1 point
- Voice Class: First or second semester, 1 block; 1 point
- Orchestra: Full year, 3 blocks; 2 points
- Piano: First and/or second semester, 3 blocks; 2 or 4 points
- Recorder Ensemble: Full year, 1 block; 1 point
- Witchmen (male chorus): Full year, 3 blocks; 2 points

Theory and Literature Courses
- Counterpoint: Full year, 1 block; 1 point. Prerequisite: Harmony or instructor's permission. The goal is to familiarize the student with contrapuntal writing through listening, analyzing, and writing. Basic counterpoint in two or three parts is stressed to acquaint the student with canons, inventions, and fugues.
- Harmony: Full year, 1 block; 1 point. Prerequisite: Music Major or equivalent. The purpose of this course is to familiarize the student with four-part writing. Creative composition, listening, analyzing, and taking chordal dictation are stressed.
- History of Music: Full year, 3 blocks; 2 points. Prerequisite: Concurrent enrollment in "Shapers of the World." This course explores the form and development of music. Recordings, films, discussions, guest artists, and field trips will familiarize students with the following musical areas: early musical forms and folk music and early classical and

commercial music (first semester); Romantic, impressionistic, and contemporary music and new musical forms and experiments (second semester).

Electronic Music Courses

- Electronic Music I: First and/or second semester, 3 times a week; 1 or 2 points. Students create music through the use of tape recorders and synthesizers. No knowledge of a musical instrument is necessary for this course. One additional block to work on projects is scheduled for each student in the music lab in lieu of homework.
- Electronic Music II: First and/or second semester, 3 times a week; 1 or 2 points. Prerequisite: Electronic Music or permission of teacher. In this course students work with synthesizers and computers on creative composition with mixed media. One additional block to work on projects in the music lab is scheduled for each student in lieu of homework.

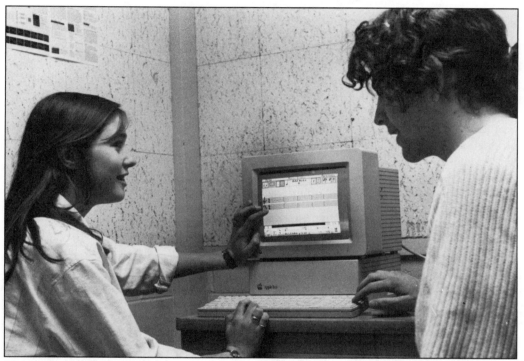

The computer in Electronic Music

Specialty Courses

- Music Major: Full year, 3 blocks; 2 points. Music Major is designed for beginning students of music. Reading, theory, ear training, and creative writing are integrated throughout the course.
- Senior Seminar: Full year, 3 blocks; 4 points. This course provides students with an opportunity to pursue their interests in music from an interdisciplinary perspective.
- Honors Music Major: Full year, 6 blocks; 4 points. Can also be taken for 3 blocks; 2 points. Prerequisite: Completion of Music Major with a grade of B or better or permission of teacher. Areas of study include sight singing, music dictation, harmonic dictation, keyboard harmony, counterpoint, stylistic writing, and creative composition. Opportunities for independent study projects for credit are available.

THE ELECTRONIC MUSIC PROGRAM

Today's music educators can no longer ignore the impact that technology has made on education and on people's understanding of music. One of the more popular electives in the general music program is Electronic Music, which introduces the latest in music technology. This program is now in its twenty-first year.

The goal of the program is to provide an environment and experiences whereby students can explore and experiment with sound in meaningful ways. Students are assisted in developing proficiency with electronic equipment, producing original projects, notating music, listening intelligently to music, developing and using a music vocabulary, understanding the evolving culture of the twenty-first century, and becoming familiar with the role music has played and continues to play in society.

Electronic Music I: This course attempts to enable students to operate and understand the functions of a tape deck, a mixer, a sequencer, an electronic keyboard, and drum synthesizers; to be able to work independently in the electronic music lab; and to respect and be responsible for the equipment while working in the lab. Students learn how to create sound using MIDI (Musical Instrument Digital Interface) equipment, learn about the technical vocabulary of electronic music, and become familiar with the works of professional musicians and performers.

The course provides students with a broad exposure to the musical capabilities of electronic equipment. It also provides them with an opportunity to explore and experiment with sound in a creative way. Specific projects (assignments) build students' confidence in their creativity as well as in their technical skills.

The students have the opportunity to work with expensive, sophisticated equipment in groups, individually, or with a partner. The course provides for individual flexibility geared to meet each student's capabilities and encourages independence, self-motivation, and self-evaluation. Books, magazines, filmstrips, videos, recordings, and films are included for inspiration and stimulation of creativity and for discussion.

The course is supplemented with demonstrations and lectures by professional artists, career and school counseling on an informal basis, and notification of concerts and performances in which electronic equipment is used. Also, students have an opportunity to present their work in class, in school, in the community, and at state and national conferences.

Grades are weighted as follows: participation and attitude in class—25 percent; attendance in class—15 percent; projects, tests, and quizzes—50 percent; and homework—10 percent.

An Electronic Music I class

Electronic Music II: Students in Electronic Music II learn to operate and understand the functions of all electronic equipment, including several synthesizers and computers; to work independently in the electronic/computer lab; and to respect and be responsible for equipment while working in the lab. Furthermore, they learn how to use equipment technically and creatively and how to work with mixed media, and they become familiar with the works of professional musicians and performers.

This course provides students with a broad exposure to the latest and most advanced electronic equipment and programs and with an opportunity to explore, experiment, and develop musical projects that incorporate other art forms (such as film, video, dance, and drama). It also gives them a chance to study historical and technical development in electronic and computer music. The course encourages independence, self-motivation, and self-evaluation and allows for individual differences. Listening and discussion provide students with the opportunity to take a leadership role.

Course materials include books, magazines, filmstrips, videos, recordings, and films for stimulation and inspiration of creativity and for discussion. The hardware used for the course consists of synthesizers, mixers, sequencers, tape decks, computers, and other equipment relevant to studio work. *Deluxe Music Construction Set, Music Studio,* and *Master Tracks* are the basic software programs that the students use for creative composition, but there are several other software programs available to the students.

The course is supplemented with demonstrations and lectures by professional artists, career and school counseling on an informal basis, and notification of concerts and performances in which electronic equipment is used. Also, students have the opportunity to present their work in class, in school, in the community, and at state, national, and international conferences.

Grades are calculated as follows: participation and attitude in class—25 percent; attendance in class—15 percent; projects, tests, and quizzes—50 percent; and homework—10 percent.

WHO SIGNS UP FOR ELECTRONIC MUSIC?

Most often, it is the nonperforming student who is interested in the latest technological developments. Some students may have synthesizers at home but may not be able to play them the way they have heard them played by rock keyboard players. These students can neither program the keyboard nor understand the functions of the various buttons, knobs, and slide switches. They are, however, familiar with equipment advertised in keyboard and guitar magazines, and they spend hours in music stores playing electronic keyboards, drum machines, guitars, and horns and appraising equalizers, sequencers, various foot pedals, and modifiers. These students plan for the day when they will have accumulated enough money to buy a sophisticated piece of equipment for themselves and they will be successful, if not famous, performing in a "group."

It always surprises these students to discover that the fundamentals of music are an important part of electronic music. Even though drum machines have preset patterns that they can hear by pushing a button and keyboards (with sequencers) can store information and play it back immediately, students become frustrated when, after "playing around" for hours on the equipment, they realize that they need more technical understanding and musical growth to further their desire to perform.

Most of the students in electronic music did not participate in any performing groups in junior high school and do not participate in any in senior high school. They did not select chorus, and yet these same young people are the vocalists in rock groups. They have the distinct feeling that "their music" is not part of the music taught at school. Only in electronic music classes can they find a bond with the material they are learning in the classroom. They learn that they can apply their schoolwork to their world of music.

Students are also surprised at the time it takes to create a three-minute composition in which they can take pleasure and pride. It is exciting to watch their progress as they combine their technical and emerging musical understandings in a compositional project. Whether the project combines electronic sounds with poetry, drama, video, or traditional instruments; is electronic alone; or is rock, abstract, pop, or classical, the objective is to provide a positive musical experience for all students.

CHANGING ROLES

Challenge is certainly a key word in electronic music—a subject that has been invaded by challenging technology. Often nonperforming students have extensive technical knowledge and can use the equipment easily. Their understanding of the latest MIDI synthesizers and computers can surpass the teacher's ability to keep up with the latest developments and changes. In such a situation, the leadership role can shift from teacher to student.

If the teacher does not understand recent technological developments, a student can take the leadership role in the classroom by demonstrating how the latest piece of equipment functions. Some teachers may feel threatened, whereas others relax and enjoy their new roles as learners and ask questions along with the class. These challenges create an environment of high energy and positive feelings.

A student demonstration in Electronic Music II

EQUIPMENT

A music teacher can start a basic MIDI lab with a limited budget and have a successful program. Equipment already available in schools, including tape recorders and tape decks, record player amplifiers, microphones, and headphones, can all be used. Simple projects using tape techniques can be initiated before the MIDI equipment arrives.

Before purchasing equipment, be sure to investigate all options thoroughly. There are many excellent products available for a MIDI lab. Keep in mind that prices will vary with dealers and that equipment is constantly being updated. Readily available devices using the MIDI standard, including keyboards, drum machines, sequencers, and computers, are all able to "talk to each other" regardless of their brand names.

If a computer is available, add the following equipment: one MIDI interface (approximately $150) for MIDI connections and synchronization, and one MIDI sequencer software program (approximately $250) for composing, storing, and editing music.

MIDI labs can vary in sophistication, depending on the budget provided; the consideration here is for the average and not for the exceptional. Consider outfitting a MIDI lab in the following stages, which should fit into a limited school budget (the costs outlined here are approximate):
- Phase 1. The school should obtain one MIDI keyboard ($750). These keyboards normally feature sixty-one touch-sensitive, full-size keys; are polyphonic (can play eight voices at the same time) and polytimbral (can play several different timbres at the same time); have

many preset voices and can store additional voices in random-access memory (RAM) cartridges; and have built-in MIDI terminals for connection to other equipment.

- Phase 2. In Phase 2 the school would purchase a sequencer ($250), two amplifier/speaker sets ($160), and MIDI cables and audio connectors ($200).
- Phase 3. Phase 3 involves the purchase of one drum machine ($250) and one MIDI expander ($100).
- Phase 4. In Phase 4, a four-track cassette recorder is purchased ($450).
- Phase 5. Purchase an eight-voice generator—basically, a synthesizer that accepts MIDI control data but has no keyboard controller of its own ($500).

SAMPLE LESSON PLANS

The following lesson plans are designed to be used as a spiraling series. Each of these "foundation" lessons requires one class session for presentation. Students will require varying amounts of time for practice and understanding.

Lesson Plan 1

Purpose:
- To review note and rest values and their relationship
- To introduce "step write" (entry of notes one at a time, defining the step size or duration of each note) on the drum machine

Conceptual understanding:
- Note and rest values in a specified meter signature

Materials:
- Drum machine
- Traditional percussion instruments

Procedure:
- Have the students clap, move to, and chant changing rhythm patterns written with graphic symbols, such as vertical lines arranged under a sequence of numbers on the chalkboard
- Translate the lines into note and rest values
- Introduce African rhythm patterns (these can be found in many works on ethnomusicology and multicultural music education, and on many recordings of African music) and discuss accent
- Clap and chant African rhythm patterns
- Play African patterns on the drum machine
- Introduce and demonstrate "step write" mode on the drum machine
- Record African rhythm patterns using step write on drum machine
- Divide class into groups, and ask each group to create a pattern using step write. Over time, give all students hands-on experience with the drum machine

Vocabulary: accent, dynamic level, monophonic rhythm, dot display, step write

Lesson Plan 2

Purpose:
- To introduce track synchronization, called simul sync (for "simultaneous synchronization") or sel sync (for "selective synchronization") by some manufacturers of tape decks. It allows the user to synchronize the material on different tracks of a tape deck.

Materials:
- Drum machine
- 4-track tape deck with simul sync
- Patch cords

Procedure:
- Record drum pattern 1 onto track 1 of the tape deck
- Introduce the synchronization controls on the tape deck and discuss the use of synchronization in recording

- Select the synchronization circuit for track 1, and record drum pattern 2 onto track 2 of tape deck
- Put track 1 back into its normal monitoring mode, and listen to tracks 1 and 2 for synchronization
- Select the synchronization circuits for tracks 1 and 2, and record drum pattern 3 onto track 3 of the tape deck
- Put tracks 1 and 2 back into normal monitoring mode, and listen to tracks 1, 2, and 3 for synchronization
- Select the synchronization circuits for tracks 1, 2, and 3, and record drum pattern 4 onto track 4 of the tape deck
- Put tracks 1, 2, and 3 back into their normal monitoring mode, and listen to tracks 1, 2, 3, and 4 for synchronization

Vocabulary: contrasting patterns, polyphonic rhythms, repetition, simul sync

Lesson Plan 3

Purpose:
- Understanding the function of the sequencer and its capabilities of responding immediately and accurately when recording
- Understanding the editing and combining functions of the sequencer, especially "trackdown" (combining the MIDI records of various tracks of musical material on the sequencer) by mixing four tracks to one

Materials:
- MIDI keyboard synthesizer
- MIDI sequencer
- Amplifier
- Speakers
- MIDI and audio patch cords

Procedure:
- Play a melody on the MIDI keyboard, recording it on the sequencer's track 1
- Transfer melody to track 2
- Play countermelody on MIDI keyboard, recording it on the sequencer's track 1
- Transfer the countermelody to track 2
- Play chords on MIDI keyboard, recording them on the sequencer's track 1

Traditional and electronic instruments in Electronic Music II

- Transfer the chords to track 2
- Play back track 2, listening to all of the stored musical information

Vocabulary: Exchange, delete, MIDI patching, sequencer, trackdown

Lesson Plan 4

Purpose:

- To create an eight-measure composition on the computer
- To introduce the capabilities of a software program
- To demonstrate how this software can be an advantage for students who do not have keyboard facility

Procedure:

- Choose a key signature and meter signature
- Write an appropriate number of chords per measure
- Create a melody above the chords; incorporate passing tones
- Experiment with timbre changes
- Listen to the melody in different keys
- Give composition a title, and save it on disk

Vocabulary: Boot, data disk, disk drive, floppy disk, hardware, load, master disk, menu, mouse, scroll, software, timbre, transpose

PROJECTS AND ASSIGNMENTS

Many projects are assigned to the students in the electronic music classes. The class is introduced to a specific piece of equipment, they follow up with a short assignment that is considered an exercise, and finally, they work on a musical project. Assignments have included writing a commercial, creating a musical scenario to a poem, creating music for a one-act play, writing music for excerpts from William Shakespeare and Kurt Vonnegut, taking a scene from the Bible and creating a sound track, creating an underwater or space odyssey, and creating music for a painting, slide, or video.

For example, during the first semester of the Honors Music Major course, the students learn to write four-part chorales. Those students who do not have keyboard facility realize their chorales on the computer, where they can hear all the voices—not fragments of sound as they struggle at the keyboard to hear their work. These students use either Music Construction Set or Music Studio. Both programs are inexpensive. Students are encouraged by their success and continue to write because they are excited about this new venture in creative composition.

The students then transpose their work for other instruments. As the composer, the student rehearses his or her work with friends who play in either the orchestra or band. The composer's suggestions usually involve recommendations for tempi, dynamic levels, and so forth; the performers make suggestions to the composer for changes because of range or difficulty in playing certain passages. This has proven to be an excellent learning experience for all involved.

The second semester of the course includes analyzing and writing canons, an invention, and a fugue in the style of Bach. Again, those students who are not keyboard players incorporate their work onto the computer, then transpose it for other instruments.

The electronic music students work in a similar format, in which they are introduced to melody and chords and realize their work on the computer. As they advance, they write their music on a sequencer software program called *Masterworks*. Many students plan multimedia compositions: combining electronic instruments with traditional instruments, with dance, with video, or with a poem or a dramatic reading. They use various styles, including classical, pop, folk, jazz, and rock—the students are encouraged to write in any style they wish as they pursue independent projects.

Many students perform their compositions for school or community functions. They are often invited to create special music for members of the dance club, who enjoy creating and choreographing the electronic sounds. Students work together for interpretation and excellence in preparation for a performance. This past school year several students wrote music for school plays, including *Voices from the High School, Don't Drink the Water, Ondine, Hamlet,* and *Twelfth Night.*

By the end of the school year, all students have had some positive feedback from their creative work. The most outstanding compositions have been recognized by the class and have been selected to be presented at the composers' concert held at the end of the school year. Some of the independent compositions have included a suite for violin, viola, and cello; music for a jazz-rock ensemble; a folk song for soprano and guitar; and a trio for trombones. One student wrote for full orchestra and had the privilege of hearing his work performed by the Greenwich Symphony Orchestra at a children's concert.

DEVELOPING MUSIC-LISTENING SKILLS

As a springboard for their own compositional experiences, students hear, discuss, and evaluate various professional recordings of such varied musicians and performers as the Police, Jethro Tull, Elton John, the Beatles, Frank Zappa, Tangerine Dream, John Cage, Edgard Varèse, Philip Glass, and Steve Reich. Modest Mussorgsky's *Pictures at an Exhibition* and Gustav Holst's *The Planets* have also been included.

On listening day the teacher and students share the direction of the class. One of the objectives is to expand students' awareness by introducing them to several composers who were influential in the development of electronic music. The teacher can share with the students classical records that have been performed on electronic equipment and have the students listen to, discuss, and evaluate both performance media. Another objective is for students to listen to and discuss the elements that are part of a musical composition (such as melody, rhythm, harmony, instrumentation, and balance). To help build a music vocabulary, musical understanding, and musical judgment, extensive musical debate is encouraged during the listening sessions.

EVALUATION

In addition to compositional and performance experiences, students are expected to develop knowledge about equipment, terminology, and musical concepts. Periodic written tests are administered.

After each session in which new equipment is introduced, students answer five to ten questions. They write and then give their answers orally without handing in their papers. This gives them an opportunity to check for incorrect answers. It is also an opportunity for them to determine whether they understand the lesson and, if not, to further question the teacher.

"Pop" quizzes constitute another opportunity for students to check their understanding. While still working on a project using the specific equipment that was introduced, the students are once again questioned. This time they pass in the papers, which the teacher grades and returns. There is more discussion, during which the students' questions are answered.

Comprehensive tests that evaluate knowledge accumulated over time are administered at the end of various grading periods. The accompanying test is an example of the type that is given at the end of the semester. It encompasses all of the material introduced, discussed, and used in projects by the students.

Students evaluate the course: The primary concern in this course is to create a classroom environment that is favorable for effective teaching and learning. This can be accomplished best through a realistic program of cooperative evaluation. Ten weeks into the course the students are asked to critique the course constructively. Through this involvement, the students take a leadership role for continuous improvement in developing objectives that are meaningful for them. A primary concern of this program is to help students improve their musical understanding and their effectiveness as musicians and as students. This can be accomplished by using mutually established goals. Self-evaluation is an integral part of the program. Open discussion, self-expression, and personal musical needs that will result in the improvement of instruction are encouraged by the teacher.

Electronic Music I—Final Exam

Match the definitions with the answers. Write the letter of your answer in the blank.
(*Note:* answers in brackets would be listed separately, preceded by letters.)

1. An electronic instrument capable of producing, modifying, and controlling sound. [synthesizer]
2. A signal fed into a circuit. [input]
3. An electronic device that generates a signal (sound). [oscillator]
4. An electronic instrument that uses a screen to display a graphic representation of a signal in the shape of a wave form. [oscilloscope]
5. Connecting cables used to link synthesizers with other components. [patch cords]
6. An electronic component designed to alter a signal in a specific way. [modifier]
7. A device that combines two or more sounds. [mixer]
8. The panoramic movement of sound; moving sound from one speaker to another. [pan]
9. A device that controls the volume or loudness of a sound. [amplifier]
10. Produces every sound we hear. [vibrations]
11. Sounds that are smooth and pure and have no overtones. [sine waves]
12. The attack, decay, sustain, and release of a wave form [envelope].
13. The tone color of a sound. [timbre]
14. The number of cycles per second of a sound wave. [frequency]
15. One complete vibration of a wave form. [cycle]
16. The basic pitch of a note. [fundamental]
17. A series of sound reflections from all surfaces between the sound source and the ear. [reverberation]
18. A wave consisting of a fundamental with all the odd-numbered harmonics. [square wave]
19. Overtones that give a tone a particular timbre. [harmonics]
20. The height of a wave form; a characteristic of sound that determines its loudness. [amplitude]
21. The initial fading of a sound. [decay]
22. Term for cycles per second. [hertz]
23. Produced by frequency. [pitch]
24. Vibrations below the audible range. [subaudio]
25. Vibrations above the audible range. [ultrasonic]
26. Squealing sound from sending the output back to the input. [feedback]
27. The distinct repetition of a sound. [echo]
28. Tone control that enables the user to control the timbre balance accurately. [equalizer]
29. Degrees of relative loudness. [dynamic levels]
30. Random combination of all frequencies in the audio spectrum. [noise]
31. A device that allows certain frequencies of a signal to pass. [filter]
32. A switch on a tape recorder that allows recorded material and source material to be synchronized. [simul sync]
33. A meter that indicates the recording or playback volume of a sound. [VU meter]
34. To listen to a sound being recorded. [monitor]
35. The first head on a tape recorder. [erase]
36. Made of polyester, acetate, and a metal or oxide coating. [recording tape]
37. Speed of a composition. [tempo]
38. Organization of musical time, often of the durations of musical sounds and silences. [rhythm]
39. In musical composition, often defined as "thin" or "thick." [texture]
40. Any simultaneous combination of sound; synonymous with chord. [harmony]
41. A change from one key signature to another. [transposition]
42. A succession of musical tones. [melody]
43. Set minimum note length (an example is if you set a sixteenth note on the drum machine as the shortest note). [quantize]
44. Visual indicator on the synthesizer. The abbreviation for light emitting diode. [LED]
45. Used as an aid in synchronizing material to be recorded in real time. [click track]
46. Circuitry used to store information. [memory]
47. An instrument that can play more than one note at a time. [polyphonic]
48. A synthesizer that can play back several timbres (presets) at one time. [polytimbral]
49. A current and popular noise reduction system. [Dolby]
50. The term used for Musical Instrument Digital Interface; it allows various synthesizers and computers to "talk to each other." [MIDI]

We try to make all students feel that they have had a part in evaluating the course throughout the school year and that they have the opportunity to make suggestions regarding its direction.

Where are the graduates? Many Greenwich graduates have stated that their success is the result of a stimulating musical environment that encouraged them and got them involved, and many have chosen music as a career. One former student sent us this comment: "Guess who's making a living playing synths…. I started as a studio assistant and now I compose scores for TV and radio. Thanks for the start, really!"

Another wrote that "My film was just released on videocassette and I'm doing a ballet-opera for January 1990. My Dickens show also won a grand prize in a California Festival this summer…. If you ever want me to come in and talk to one of your classes, let me know. I'd love to!" A Japanese student who studied with us mentioned that his friends "were quite interested in the kind of music that I was doing and were saying that they wished they had such facilities in their high schools."

General music classes that involve students in creative composition capitalize on the needs of the students to be actively involved. They challenge students to learn to think, to wonder, to be wrong, or to be right. They also encourage students to become socially interactive through productive participation in a nonthreatening environment. Such courses as those at Greenwich High School that make use of electronic equipment are very effective, since the interest of many of the students in this medium is especially acute—many even own electronic keyboards. Involvement with electronic instruments provides an outlet for creative expression through performance. The student faces the dilemma of every composer in his or her attempt to manipulate sound in a meaningful manner in experiences that encourage continued, self-directed growth beyond the high school years.

Goals and Rationale: This course seeks to involve participating students in a survey of music from different world cultures and from varying historical periods. Emphasis is placed on enhancing student growth in the elements of music through the use of creative, hands-on compositional techniques growing out of the study of individual and collective musical elements.

Program Requirements: Equipment used in this program includes percussion instruments, such as conga drums, woodblocks, claves, Orff-type xylophones, cowbells, and two-tone bells; synthesizers, such as the Time Lab from I. W. Turner and the Roland Juno 6; guitars, both full and 3/4 size; an old acoustic piano used as a prepared piano; cassette and reel-to-reel tape recorders; and a stereo (including headphones for individual listening).

CHAPTER 10

Small-Group Learning

by Jeannette M. Hall

Marysville, Washington, is a middle-class, suburban community near Seattle. The school system consists of one high school (10–12), one junior high school (8–9), and one middle school (6–7). Each school provides educational experiences for approximately 1,200 students.

One credit in fine arts is required for graduation from Marysville Junior High School. Consequently, the music program offers elective general music instruction designed primarily for nonperformance students. This course focuses on providing participants with an opportunity to study the elements of music by using media such as synthesizers and related electronic equipment, guitars, drums, and other percussion instruments. Students are actively involved in learning about an element of music by studying its treatment in the compositions of master composers and music from divergent world cultures. They also have an opportunity to increase their understanding of each element by creating their own compositions using elements being studied.

COURSE DOCUMENTATION

Emphasis in this course is placed on involving students in laboratory experiences with music. The general music curriculum is divided into four areas: orientation, "ear cleaning" and "ear stretching," sample groups and stations, and the final project. The orientation focuses on group activities, including listening, demonstration of equipment, lectures and discussions regarding musical elements, and reading rhythm patterns. Throughout the orientation process, emphasis is placed on students recognizing how each topic will be used later in the semester in their own compositions. The entire orientation period serves to broaden students' ideas about the nature of music.

The ear cleaning and stretching process is inserted at appropriate times throughout the semester. Students are provided with opportunities to listen to recordings of music from such diverse sources as Thomas Morley madrigals, Balinese *gamelan* works, the indeterminacy of John Cage, and the hocket technique of some Pygmy peoples. They can also use listening

CONTACT: *Jeannette M. Hall, music teacher, Marysville Junior High School, 1605 Seventh Street, Marysville, WA 98270.*

stations in the music lab for more musical exposure. Each experience enhances students' concepts of music and their awareness of common elements in music throughout the world.

Experiences in sample groups constitute the bulk of the curriculum. Each class is given the opportunity to divide itself into eight groups (A–H). The room is arranged into learning stations, and station assignments are provided for each class period.

Each group is asked to complete one or two stations per class period. Upon entering the classroom, students note their assigned stations. In one class period, groups A and B might complete two assignments, spending alternate halves of the class at a listening station and at a synthesizer, while groups C and D combine for the entire period to work on the Marimba 1 station. The next day, groups rotate to new stations; it takes four class periods to rotate through the separate stations. After completing the cycle of stations, the class comes back together and shares ideas, experiences, and questions, and students perform for each other. Teacher lecture and/or demonstration is an important part of this stage of instruction.

There are seven sets of stations that are themselves rotated throughout the semester. The stations use the following equipment (students are also encouraged to bring in and use additional materials for various station assignments):

> *Set 1:* I. W. Turner Time Lab/Listening 1; Marimba 1; Drumming 1; Guitar or *Kalimba*
>
> *Set 2:* Marimba 2; Tape Loop 1/Drumming 2; Guitar or *Kalimba*; I. W. Turner synthesizer 2/ Listening
>
> *Set 3:* Prepared Piano 1/Tape Loop 2; Guitar or *Kalimba*; I. W. Turner synthesizer 3/Listening; Marimba 3
>
> *Set 4:* Guitar or *Kalimba*; I. W. Turner Time Lab 4/Listening; Marimba 4; Prepared Piano 2; Drumming 3
>
> *Set 5:* I. W. Turner Time Lab 5/Listening; Marimba 5; Guitar or *Kalimba*; Prepared Piano 2; Drumming 3
>
> *Set 6:* Marimba 6; Guitar or *Kalimba*; Slide Show; Prepared Piano 3; Roland synthesizer 1/ Listening
>
> *Set 7:* Guitar or *Kalimba*; Roland synthesizer 2/Listening; Slide Show; Prepared Piano; Marimba 7

LAB ASSIGNMENTS

At each station, specific directions, assignments, comments, and appropriate supporting materials are included in "direction folders." Samples of these directions appear in the accompanying examples. The directions in each folder begin with the instruction, "Read and follow these instructions carefully" and end with *"Work quietly!"*

Drumming. The three drumming lessons build toward the group's performance of an original composition.

Drumming 1
Your combined groups have the entire period to complete the assignment.

Assignment: Prepare one of the drumming scores for your group to play in front of the rest of the class.

Requirements and process:
1. Practice quietly! This room is not soundproof.
2. If you use sticks, be sure to grab them with the taped side in your hand.
3. If you need more stools, try the marimba room or use a chair from the classroom.
4. Decide which score you would like to work on. This may involve trying each of them before you finally decide.
5. Keep your plans simple. Start out with only one or two parts, and add parts as you can handle them. Make your performance only as difficult as you can manage—it is better to have it simple and successful than a complicated mess.
6. Decide who is going to play what parts. No one should have a part that is overwhelming. You will find that you will fall apart under the pressure of performance unless you are entirely confident of your part in rehearsal.

7. Use variety. You don't all have to actually use drums. In fact, you could play any score on any combination of instruments or even do some changing during your piece.

8. There are some things you must agree on before performing your piece. You are very much advised to write these down so that when you are in front of the class, your performance appears very well prepared. Consider the following: Who plays which instruments? What sticks do you use? How long will your performance last? How will it begin? How will it end? What will be your seating arrangement in performance?

9. Be careful with the equipment. When you are finished, put everything back as you found it *or better*. Make sure any drums you used are back in their proper sacks. Once in the bags, the drums are to be stored upside down.

Drumming 2

Your group has half the period to complete this assignment.

Assignment: Begin work on an original composition. (You will have one more full class period to complete your composition and be ready to perform for the class.)

Requirements and process:

1. Your piece should be in a style similar to that of the drum pieces you have already learned, using ostinatos.

2. Take about ten minutes to "fool around." Someone will soon come upon a pattern that can be used.

3. Once someone has found a pattern, everyone must learn it.

4. Now, devise a way to write it down. This may be a chart of numbers or symbols, or it could be a system of your own invention.

5. When time is called, put your score in your group folder and see to it that *all* of the equipment is put away properly.

Remember: Practice quietly; if you use sticks, be sure to grab them with the taped side in your hand; and *keep your ostinato to a level of difficulty that everyone in your group can handle.*

Students drumming

Drumming 3

Your group has the entire period to complete this assignment.

Assignment: Finish your drum composition so that it is ready to perform for the class, and prepare a score on the 18" x 24" score paper.

Requirements and process:

1. Get the score of your earlier ostinato from your group folder and review it.

2. Your performance may have only one ostinato, but if you would like another one, here's what to do: While one or two persons play the original ostinato, someone else fools around until he or she discovers a pattern that goes with the original pattern.

3. There is no reason you can't add a third ostinato if you have three people in your group, but keep your performance only as difficult as you can handle.

4. Watch the time. Before you leave, you need to have completed your score. Your written score is 50 percent of your grade—make sure it is complete. Consider and note: Who plays which instruments? What sticks do you use? How long will your performance last? How will it begin? How will it end? What will be your seating arrangement in performance?

5. When time is called, put your score on the grand piano and see to it that *all* of the equipment is put away properly.

Prepared Piano. The three prepared piano lessons start with the invention of sounds for the medium and work toward a multilayered piece with ostinatos and improvisation.

Prepared Piano 1

You have half the period to complete this assignment.

Assignment: Experiment with sounds that you can get from this instrument.

Requirements and process:

1. Work carefully so that you don't damage the instrument or endanger yourself.

2. *Work quietly.* Your biggest problem at this station is being too loud. *Do not* disturb the other people in the room.

3. Work slowly and avoid dropping any of the items inside the piano. They are hard to get out.

4. Challenge yourself to use a variety of objects, placed in a variety of locations.

5. When time is up, remove all of your preparations so that the next group has a fresh start.

6. If you discover any sounds worth remembering, start noting them on a sheet called "Prepared Piano Sounds Worth Keeping." Make an effort to find some sounds worth saving—your next Prepared Piano assignment will require them. If you do note any sounds, put the paper in your group folder.

Students playing prepared piano

Prepared Piano 2

You have the entire period to complete this assignment.

Assignment: Compose a four- to twelve-note ostinato for the prepared piano, and write it down.

Requirements and process:
1. Return to prepared piano sounds that you discovered last time or develop new ones. Fool around until you find a pattern worth working with. In doing this, consider both the preparation of the piano and the pattern of notes.
2. Be patient with yourselves! You may not come up with anything quickly.
3. Once you come up with an ostinato, write it down. In writing the pattern out, consider: using the numbers on the keys, using standard notation, drawing the inside of the piano, or developing a chart. When your score is complete, put it in your group folder.
4. If you have extra time, fool around in an effort to discover another ostinato that will fit with the one you just composed (you will be required to write another ostinato).
5. When time is called, clean out the piano.

Prepared Piano 3

You have the entire period to complete this assignment.

Assignment: Complete your Prepared Piano piece by composing a second ostinato, which is to be played with the ostinato pattern you have already composed; make a score.

Requirements and process:
1. You must come up with two counterpoint ostinato patterns, notated in a complete score and presented in a class performance.
2. Get your rough score of your earlier ostinato and review playing it.
3. While someone in your group continues to play the ostinato, the others should fool around or improvise until at least one person comes up with a new ostinato that fits with the original pattern.
4. Remember, this piece is to be for Prepared Piano, so some, but not necessarily all, of your sounds must be "prepared" sounds (you can also play inside the instrument).
5. Again, be patient.
6. Finish your score before time is called. Make sure it is complete (check the classroom poster on the elements of a complete score). Your score may be in any form: a drawing, a graph, traditional notation, numbers, or a chart. Be creative.
7. Rehearse your performance so that you are ready to perform for the class.
8. When you are finished, turn in your score and "unprepare" the piano.

Options:
1. If you have three people in your group, have two players handle the two ostinatos and have the third player improvise. Just make sure you can really pull this off: improvisation is not something that takes the place of doing your assignment.
2. Prepared Piano lends itself nicely to *programmatic ideas.* Does one of you have a story to tell?
3. If your second ostinato comes to you easily, there is no reason you can't have a third or even a fourth.
4. Your composition can include other instruments if you have sufficient time for planning.

Marimba. In their work at the marimba stations, the students get an introduction to the music of another culture by playing two marimba pieces of the Shona people of Zimbabwe, Africa. (A third, optional piece is available for those students who have the time.) The students also compose and notate their own music in the Shona style.

In the first four lessons on the marimba, the students use the accompanying handout. They are not given an actual score to the pieces—this music is from an oral tradition, and I maintain that tradition in teaching it. The basic pattern of this piece is taught to the class as a whole before they take it to the stations. The notation on the handout is simply a reminder to students of the note names.

Marimba lessons five, six, and seven are devoted to writing an original marimba piece, devising an appropriate notation, and preparing it for performance.

Marimba 1

Your groups have the entire period to work on this assignment. (If you truly find your combined groups are just too many people, you can be separated, but the piece is best with at least four performers or more.)

Assignment: Prepare the marimba piece "Kukaiwa" (the title translates as "Don't Bother Me") for a class performance. You will have two times at this station before you will perform for the class.

Requirements and process:

1. Use the instruction sheet to help you with the notes. (See accompanying figure.)
2. Start your practice with the basic pattern, practicing slowly at a speed the whole group can handle.
3. Help each other. Each person in the group must participate. If you have any questions, send someone out for help.
4. Keep it simple—better simple and together than complicated and a mess!
5. Write down who is playing what so that you can remember next time.
6. Be careful with the equipment. If you are crowded, place the marimbas you are not using just outside the marimba room door.
7. When you are finished, put everything back as you found it or better!

African Marimba Songs
Shona Tribe, from Zimbabwe

"Kukaiwa"
   Basic pattern:
   C/G x 6   A/F x 6 (question)
   C/G x 6   G/E x 6 (answer)

   Start = six *hosho* shakes in tempo

"Rugare"
   Basic pattern:

right hand	C	C	C	E	E	D	D	D	(question)
left hand	G	G	G	C	C	A	A	A	
right hand	C	C	C	D	D	C	C	C	(answer)
left hand	G	G	G	A	A	G	G	G	

   Start = eight *hosho* shakes in tempo

"Chiradza"
   Basic pattern:

| *right hand* | G | | E C C C D C G | | E C C C B C | (question) |
| *left hand* | | G | G G G A G | | G | G G G G G | (answer) |

   Start = either lead drum or marimba
   Shangara drum beat:
   R L R L R L R R L R R L

Handout for Marimba Lesson 1

Marimba 5

   Your groups have the entire period to work on this assignment. This complete project will include three times at this station.

Assignment: Compose an ostinato pattern in the style of the Shona marimba music and devise a way to write it down.

Requirements and process:

1. The creative process for this piece usually begins by fooling around. Most of you, in time, will hit on something worth sharing. Take ten minutes to fool around.
2. Share each others' ideas. Show each other your patterns, and decide which pattern you want to use.
3. Modify the pattern if necessary. You may want to use the original pattern as a starting point and then change it to improve or vary it. (If at this point, you don't really have a good pattern or the one you were first working with is falling apart, go back to step one.)

4. Once you have a basic ostinato that pleases you, everyone should learn the pattern. Remember to keep your basic pattern simple enough for everyone to play: later, there will be room for more complicated parts.
5. Devise a notation for the pattern and get it on paper.
6. If time allows, work on variations of your pattern.
7. When time is called, put your score in your group folder.
8. Be very careful with the equipment. Remember, if you are too crowded, you can place the marimbas you are not using just outside the marimba room door.
9. When you are finished, put everything back as you found it or better.

Marimba 6

Your groups have the entire period to work on this assignment.

Assignment: Compose an ostinato pattern in counterpoint to the ostinato that you composed last time.

Requirements and process:
1. Get your score of your earlier ostinato and review the part. *Everyone* needs to be able to play this basic part.
2. While one or two people in your group continue to play the ostinato, the others are to improvise or fool around until at least one person comes up with a new ostinato that fits with the original pattern.
3. Take your time. You have the whole period to compose this second ostinato and get it written out.
4. Each person in your group will need to be patient with all the other group members—you must work together.
5. The following are some general rules for this composition: All notes C, E, and G go together; the notes A, F, and D go together.
6. Before time is called, notate your two ostinatos. The score will be 50 percent of your grade for this assignment.
7. If your second ostinato comes very easily, there is no reason you can't add a third or even a fourth one.
8. When time is called, put your score in your group folder.
9. Be very careful with the equipment. Again, if you are too crowded, you can place the marimbas you are not using just outside the marimba room door.
10. When you are finished, put everything back as you found it or better.

You will have one more time at this station to work on this composition and finish it before you play it for the class. If you have time, review "Kukaiwa" and "Chiradza."

I. W. Turner Time Lab. At this station, students spend one session gaining control over the sounds. Sessions two and three are spent with graphic scores, first following the color and shape of lines of a given score, and then writing and recording a work based on an original graphic score. The fourth session is devoted to following a "box notation" score, and the fifth is spent in developing and recording a final composition.

I. W. Turner Time Lab 1

Your group has half the period, around twenty minutes, to complete this assignment.

Assignment: Set up at least one of the possible arrangements of the electronic music lab so that it produces sounds you can hear, and record some sounds with the tape recorder.

Requirements:
1. Each person in the group must participate.
2. Once the lab is set up, work to gain control of the sounds being produced.
3. On this assignment, you will not turn in a tape, but simply make sure each person understands how to set up and control the lab.
4. Before time is called, try to include the use of the tape recorders, too.
5. If you have questions, send out a runner.

Process:
1. Pick out one of the easier arrangements for the lab.
2. Figure out which instruments you will use.

3. Get those instruments out and put the others aside.
4. Pick out the same number of patch cords as you did instruments, and set the extra patch cords aside or leave them hanging.
5. Connect instruments to one end of the cords.
6. Connect instruments to the amplifier and turn on the amplifier. Note: The reel-to-reel tape recorder can also serve as an amplifier.
7. Experiment with the controls to gain confidence in operating the lab.
8. If you have enough time, try setting up another arrangement of the lab.
9. When time is called, everything must be in order and accounted for. Please be very careful with the instruments.
10. Make sure all of the instruments are turned off.
11. Leave the station as neat as you found it or neater!

I. W. Turner Time Lab 3

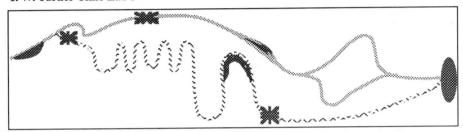

Sample student score for I. W. Turner Time Lab 3 project. The lines of different density represent different colors.

Your group has half the period, about twenty minutes, to complete this assignment.

Assignment: Create a piece of music on the tone generators (using your own score) and record it on the group tape.

Requirements:
1. You have made a tape that followed a colored score that was already made for you. Now you will make your own score and then record your piece using that score.
2. Your piece may last two minutes but no longer.
3. Each person should participate in the assignment.

Process:
1. Consider the kinds of sounds you know you can make, and figure out how you might draw the sounds.
2. The music should sound like the colors and shapes of your lines. Design your score's notation so that listeners can follow the score as they listen.
3. Plan your score. Decide how you want your piece to go.
4. Draw your score. Keep it simple, using two or three colors.
5. Set up the tape recorder so that it will be ready to record sounds from the generators.
6. Decide who is going to play which part. Each person should have a part.
7. Practice your piece. You may need a conductor to make sure that the piece is performed as planned.
8. Record your piece. Remember, if you don't use a microphone for recording, you may talk while recording.
9. Rewind the tape so that it is ready to hand in. Label the tape with its playing speed and with your group's letter, and turn in both the tape and the score.
10. Leave your station as you found it. Make sure all generators are turned off!

I. W. Turner Time Lab 4
Your group has half the period, around twenty minutes, to complete this assignment.

Assignment: Tape a piece of music using the accompanying score.

Requirements:
1. Each person in the group must participate.
2. Use the accompanying score, beginning in the upper left-hand square marked "I" and ending in either of the squares marked "E."

3. You may move from square to square horizontally or vertically, but not diagonally.
4. Spend fifteen seconds in each square.
5. Play the shaded squares loudly.

Process:

1. Make sure the lab is set up as shown below the score.
2. Set up the tape recorder so it will record the sounds from the lab.
3. Figure out exactly which way you will proceed through the squares.
4. Practice going through your piece. It will work best if each person has an instrument or two and you have someone to conduct the piece.
5. Be sure to adjust all volumes so that all instruments are balanced.
6. Record your piece at 3¾ inches per second. Your conductor can point at the square being played and keep time.
7. Label your tape properly and turn it in.
8. Leave the station neat. Make sure that all instruments are turned off!

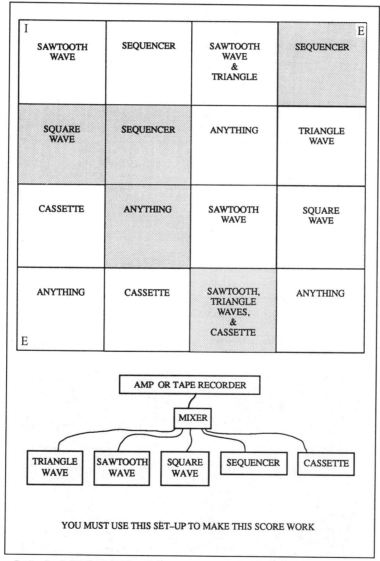

Score for I. W. Turner Time Lab 4

Kalimba. The units on *kalimba*, like those for the marimba, do not use scores in traditional notation. Instead, students are supplied with diagrams and number charts like the accompanying example, for "Kukaiwa."

R	5	8	7	5	8	6
L	3	1	1	3	1	2
R	5	8	7	5	8	6
L	3	4	1	3	4	2
R	56	88	77	56	88	66
L	3	1	1	3	1	2
R	56	88	77	56	88	66
L	3	4	1	3	4	2
R	5•	6–•	87•	5•	6–•	86•
L	•3	•1–	••1	•3•	1–	••2
R	5•	6–•	87•	5•	6–•	86•
L	•3	•4–	••1	•3•	4–	••2

Kalimba *chart of "Kukaiwa"*

Kalimba 1

You have the entire period to work with the *kalimba*.

Assignment: Learn "Kukaiwa." When this song is learned and checked off, you can plan your next selection from the other three *kalimba* songs provided.

Requirements:

1. "Kukaiwa" must be checked off in the gradebook before the seven sets of stations end.
2. Your performance needs to be smooth and must include the entire page of the accompanying chart.
3. Once you have been checked, you may either go on with the *kalimba* or proceed to the guitar.

Students playing kalimbas

Process:

1. Stay at this station until you are excused.
2. Your group can work together, you can work in groups of two, or you can work alone.
3. The *kalimba* is played with the thumbs. Each key is numbered on the chart; the numbers on the charts that are aligned vertically are played together. Where numbers on the charts are staggered, the *kalimba* keys are played alternately.
4. Do not move the keys on the *kalimba*. They will go out of tune.
5. When time is called, make sure that you put everything away as it was when you came to this station.
6. When you are ready to be checked off in the gradebook, say something. (You may not be asked.) You will be tested during your time at the *kalimba* station, not while you are at another station.
7. Practice quietly—go easy on your thumbs.
8. After finishing "Kukaiwa," continue to practice the additional songs. There are tapes available to assist you in learning these songs. If you think they might help you, request them.

FINAL PROJECTS

Once students have completed the seven sets of stations, they choose three final projects. The remainder of the semester, usually four to five weeks, is be spent on these projects. Of the three, at least one must be for class presentation, one for personal proficiency, and the third can be either. Students may choose from any of the areas in which they have already worked, but they may also choose to work on a music video, a report, a recorder, computer music theory, or instrument making.

I am constantly impressed by the students in this program. It is a rare student who doesn't know exactly what he or she wants to work on by this time. At this stage in the program, it is a real pleasure to follow them with materials and ideas and let them go!

The quality of the students' work in the final projects is a joy to be a part of. Admittedly, I get some "junk"; but, in retrospect, we recognize the process was valuable and part of the creative experience. The most personal rewards come from those students who experience little success elsewhere in the school day.

PRACTICAL CONSIDERATIONS

Enrollment: At registration, an average of seventy students request General Music. Enrollment is limited to thirty-four, which allows for eight groups of four with two student assistants. Students with special needs may be placed in the program on the advice of a counselor, but in general, students are chosen randomly (by computer) for enrollment.

Equipment: When funds are limited, instruments can be created from a variety of sound sources. Barrel drums, glass chimes from gallon jugs, rattles from gourds, coconut shells, and so forth—all have possibilities for use in the classroom. If funding is available, good-quality instruments should be used. Students appreciate experiencing sounds on high-quality instruments.

Recordings

Comparative Composition:

Pictures at an Exhibition, by Modest Musorgsky, orchestration by Maurice Ravel. Any orchestral recording.

Pictures at an Exhibition, by Modest Musorgsky, arranged by Tomita. RCA ARL I-8033. An electronic version.

Pictures at an Exhibition, by Modest Musorgsky, arranged and performed by Emerson, Lake and Palmer. Cotillion ELP 66666.

Porgy and Bess, by George Gershwin. A recording of the entire opera plus a piano/vocal score. Serves as an introduction to opera. The vocal score makes the text available to students.

Porgy and Bess, by George Gershwin, version by Ray Charles and Cleo Laine. RCA CPL2-1831.

The Rite of Spring, by Igor Stravinsky, version by Hubert Laws. CTI 6012. An example of traditional composition handled in another style.

Elements:

An American in Paris, by George Gershwin. Columbia MS 7258. For the study of form and style.

Concerto for Prepared Piano, by John Cage. Nonesuch H-71202. For the study of tone color.

Headhunters, by Herbie Hancock. Columbia KC 32731. The selection "Chameleon" can be used to demonstrate ostinato bass.

Houses of the Holy, by Led Zeppelin, Atlanta SD 7255. "The Crunge" is an example of mixed meter, useful in the study of rhythm.

New Sounds in Electronic Music. Odyssey 32-16-DI60. For the study of tone color.

The World of Harry Partch, compositions by Harry Partch. Columbia MS 7207. Examples of percussion color from instruments designed and constructed by Partch.

Paul Horn and Nexus. Epic KE 33561. Nexus is a group that uses some familiar rhythm patterns and percussion instruments.

Symphony No. 7, by Ludwig van Beethoven. Any recording. The second movement of this work has a good example of a rhythmic ostinato, and it is a good example for demonstrating the fact that large-scale works can be built on simple ideas.

Ethnomusicology:

African Story-Songs—Told and Sung by Abraham Dumisani Maraire, University of Washington Press. The selection "Tete Dzambira" is an attractive composition.

Rufaro! Dumi and the Minanzi Marimba Ensemble. Voyager VRLP 404-S. Contains marimba songs used in class.

Programmatic Compositions:

Journey to the Center of the Earth, by Rick Wakeman. A & M Sp 3621. Most students know the story. Have a copy of the book, by Jules Verne, on hand.

Miscellaneous Recordings:

Blood on the Tracks, by Bob Dylan. Columbia BL 33235. "Lily, Rosemary, and the Jack of Hearts" is a fun and complicated ballad.

Inside Paul Horn. Epic BXN 26466. This is a great album to use in focusing on acoustics.

Some Additional Programs

Classical Music and Opera is an enrichment course open to any student. In it, students become acquainted with "great music."

Contact: Donald J. Stabiler, De La Salle High School, 5300 St. Charles Avenue, New Orleans, LA 70115.

Electronic Music was named a "Program of Excellence" by the Minnesota Department of Education in 1985 and 1986 and a "Selection of Excellence" by the Minnesota Alliance for Arts in Education in 1988. The one-year course involves study of the components and technical operation of music synthesizers and other electronic equipment and investigation of the related areas of creative composition, music theory, and acoustics.

Contact: Brian Williams, Wayzata High School, 305 Vicksburg Lane, Plymouth, MN 66447.

Handbells provides students with hands-on experience in making music while providing a practical means of using knowledge and skills acquired in the course. This is a one-semester course that is open to any student.

Contact: William E. Melton, Carter High School, Route 2, Carter School Road, Strawberry Plains, TN 37871.

Keyboard Experiences is a one-semester course that is open to all students. In it, pop, sacred, and folk music styles are emphasized in a curriculum designed to teach keyboard harmony and develop the students' personal enrichment.

Contact: Marianne Holland, Spring Valley High School, Sparkleberry Lane, Columbia, SC 29223.

Music Appreciation, required of all Stuyvesant High School students not selected to participate in the Instrumental Music program, has been offered at this school since 1904. Instruction begins with music such as motion picture sound tracks and moves through musical examples from all eras.

Contact: Joseph R. Rutkowski, Stuyvesant High School, 345 East Fifteenth Street, New York, NY 10003.

Music Nine is a required arts/humanities course for all freshmen at Abraham Lincoln High School. The development of perception–music listening skill is a primary goal of the course.

Contact: Saul Feinberg, Abraham Lincoln High School, Rowland and Ryan Avenues, Philadelphia, PA 19136.

Music Spectrum affords opportunities with a variety of performance media including recorder, guitar, and keyboard. Additionally, students develop music listening skills.

Contact: Frank Pacocha, Jr., Suffield High, Mountain Road, Suffield, CT 06078.

Synthesizer is a one-semester course that has been offered for fifteen years. In it, students use the synthesizer for compositional experiences.

Contact: Jerome N. Margolis, Harvard School, 3700 Coldwater Canyon, North Hollywood, CA 91604.